CONTENTS

Reprint Series Editor – W. G. Spittal

82046

PREFACE

Long the subjects of misunderstanding and distortion in popular literature, grade-school histories and the folkloric fantasies of Hollywood the realities of Indian Scalping and Torture in North America nonetheless have been treated to scholarly examination in the three studies presented here. Until now each had been long out of print and generally inaccessible to the interested student and general reader.

While there may be accusations of sensationalism and pandering to stereotypes by the re-issue of these provocative materials the editor is of the opinion that they are valid examinations which will dispel or clarify, for Indian and non-Indian readers alike, many such charges by the documentation of the historical record surrounding these emotionally loaded topics. Was scalping of native origin? How did Europeans affect the practice? Did Indians burn captives at the stake? These subjects still incite controversy; the authors report the data as they have been recorded in the historical literature. Regrettably, the particular opposing cases of some contemporary polemicists are unlikely to be swayed by these thoughtful presentations. Perhaps the behaviour of individuals and societies might better be judged within the milieu of their own times and cultures, and judged with access to original source materials. For an example of the first portion of this proposition one need only reflect on the revolutionary changes during the past twenty years in the legal and social responses in North America towards the destruction of a live human fetus.

If these studies have a common fault it might be the lack of depth in their analysis of the cultural background, and in particular the war-complex with its religious overtones, from which these activities derived such as would be standard in the work of modern ethnologists. However, the authors were not modern ethnologists and such an expectation would demand more of them than they were trained to give. Always the reader must remember that the undeniably grizzly details of Scalping and Torture were subject to unconscious or deliberate exaggeration when interpreted through the foreign cultural biases of colonialists often at war with native populations. As well, the more gruesome the reportage the greater was its propaganda value in rallying opinion against "savages" impeding the "rightful" expansion of "Christian civilization" into the "wilderness". Francis Parkman's overdrawn racist histories offer one of the monumental examples in American historical writing of this treatment. Native activists have long both emphasized this opportunity for distortion on the part of hostile alien chroniclers, and, to balance their look at the past, reminded the modern population of past atrocities committed by Europeans not only upon native peoples but upon their fellow Europeans in the name of religion, politics, social order and racial purity. Acts of barbarism were facts of daily life in earlier times, and, if reports are to be believed from such disparate locales as Afghanistan, Chile, Iran, Kampuchia, Lebanon, Nicaraugua, Vietnam, and too many other places, not altogether unknown in our own time.

Ohsweken, Ontario. September, 1985   WGS

NOTE: Numbers at page tops are those of the original printings: consecutive numbers at
        page bottoms are those assigned to this reprint edition.

SCALPING IN AMERICA.[a]

By Georg Friederici.

I.

The habit among the American aborigines of scalping fallen enemies, and of carrying off the secured piece of skin and hair as a
trophy, was a wholly new sight to the early American voyagers and
settlers. The first edition of Herodotus, with his account of scalping
among the Scythians, appeared in 1502 and was accessible to a few of
the learned only, and ethnological information concerning other
primitive races was wanting.

The word scalp is English and originally signified a shell or
the crown of the head. Its use in the present sense is quite recent;
even well toward the end of the seventeenth century one reads only
of " skynnes with the heades and crownes," " cut off their haire round
about," " skins of those heads," " haire skulls of his enemies," " the
skin of their heads flayed off," " crowns, or haire and skinne of the
head," and similar terms. In 1675, however, Josselyn employed
" the hair-scalp," and since then the term came gradually into general use. In the beginning of the eighteenth century Lawson and
Byrd used simply scalp, or sculp. In French, German, and Dutch
writings the evolution of the term progressed also very slowly.

So far as the author could ascertain, it was Francisco de Garay
who, in 1520, made the first acquaintance with the Indian habit of
scalping. This occurred during De Garay's unfortunate expedition
to Pánuco. The accounts are, however, so brief and the procedure
was so little characteristic that only an extended knowledge of the
custom enables one to recognize a mode of scalping. It consisted in
this particular case in cutting off the skin of the entire head and

[a] Scalpieren und ähnliche Kriegsgebräuche in Amerika. Inaugural-Disserta-
tion zur Erlangung der Doktorwürde der Philosophischen Fakultät der Uni-
versität Leipzig. Vorgelet von Georg Friederici. Braunschweig, Druck von
Friedrich Vieweg und Sohn, 1906. Octavo, pp. vi, 1–172, with çolored map,
folded. Abstract, with the author's permission, of pages 1 to 76. For detailed
bibliography see the original.

face, with hair and beard, which was shown to be the habit among the Chichimecs to the regions of Jalisco and Michoacan.

The first writer who gave an account of typical Indian scalping was Jacques Cartier. During his second voyage in 1535 he was shown by the natives of Hochelaga (Montreal) five scalps of their mortal enemies, the Toudamans. These scalps were already dry and stretched on small wooden hoops. The Indians of Montreal spoke the Huron-Iroquois language.

A few years later, in 1540, the habit of scalping is met with by De Soto in the south, among tribes speaking the Muskhogean. One of De Soto's men, Simón Rodriguez, was scalped near the Appalachian Bay and his comrade Roque de Yelves barely escaped the same misfortune. Alonso de Carmona gives on this occasion the first clear account of the mode in which the Indians take the scalp and of the value the trophy has for them.

The next information concerning scalping comes from Florida, in 1549, and is soon followed by the important data of Tristán de Luna on the warlike natives of Georgia and Alabama, and of Laudonnière on those of Florida. By 1565 the reports concerning the usage present already a fairly complete picture of scalping and the various details connected with it, and this picture is made more precise through the ethnologically valuable drawings of Le Moynes, preserved by De Bry.

Meanwhile the presence of the custom was reported by Ulrich Schmidel from South America. The secretary of Cabeza de Vaca was not so well informed and speaks only of cutting off the entire head; this refers very likely to the Guaycurú-Mbayá, who, in common with all related tribes of the Chaco, first cut off the heads and then scalp them.

During the last third of the sixteenth century there are scarcely any further accounts of scalping, but the first decade of the following century shows three good reports: That of Lescarbot, from Nova Scotia; that written by Captain Smith in Virginia, and that of Champlain, dealing with the territory of the St. Lawrence. Champlain's experiences and observations are especially valuable and well show the usages connected with scalping. In 1603 this author attended a great celebration of a victory by the united Algonquin, Montagnais, and Etchemin. They had secured some Iroquois scalps and with these their women performed a scalp dance. In 1609 Champlain accompanied the united Algonquin, Montagnais, and Huron on a war expedition against the Iroquois. The battle took place in the neighborhood of the present Fort Ticonderoga and the Iroquois, who for the first time faced firearms, were defeated. Here Champlain personally witnessed, with all the other horrors of Indian warfare, the scalping of the dead and of the tortured prisoners, and he was also present at the reception of the returning victors, laden with scalps, at Tadoussac. As the flotilla of canoes neared the settlement, the women threw off their clothing and swam to the boats, where with cries of triumph they took the scalps into their care. Then followed other festivities and dances, and toward the last Champlain himself was presented with a scalp.

After Champlain the reports concerning scalping are very frequent.

II.

GEOGRAPHICAL AND CHRONOLOGICAL EXTENSION OF SCALPING—DEVELOPMENT OF THE SCALP FROM THE HEAD TROPHY—REMARKS ON HAND, EAR, AND FINGER TROPHIES.

Scalping in its commonly known form and greatest extent was, as will be shown later, largely the result of the influence of white people, who introduced firearms, which increased the fatalities in a conflict, brought the steel knife, facilitating the taking of the scalp, and finally offered scalp premiums, which so stimulated the hunt for these objects that the removing of whole heads was abandoned. It is certain that head taking preceded scalp taking and that the latter was a development from the former, induced by the inconvenience and other difficulties which attended carrying off the whole head. This is not merely a rational deduction from facts, but is confirmed in some of the old reports and by the Indians themselves, and is a logical consequence of the conception common among the Indians and many other primitive peoples that a part of the body may be equivalent to and completely represent the whole. If an enemy is killed or their own warrior dies near a settlement, then the whole body is brought over, to be maltreated to satiation in the first or receive the proper honors in the second instance. If the distance from home is greater, the body is cut into pieces that can be transported, or, if even this would be attended with difficulty, only the head and possibly a hand are brought in; while under still greater difficulties of transportation it is the jaw alone that is brought, or more commonly the scalp. This shows the signification of the scalp lock. In cases where a scalp had been taken and the head was cut off subsequently, we are confronted with a case of mutilation; such a head was never regarded as a trophy, but was maltreated and thrown away. This briefly sketched development of the practice of scalping can be followed especially well among the Algonquin.

Very good evidence for the assumption that the scalp trophy was a development of the head trophy and that the Indians were originally all head-hunters, is afforded by the native pictography. In this the scalped bodies are always represented headless.

3

The opinion is quite general that scalping was practiced by all the North American Indians, and that it did not exist in South America. Both of these notions are erroneous, for notwithstanding the fact that the habit spread greatly after the discovery of North America, yet there are immense stretches of the country where scalping was never in vogue, and on the other hand the usuage has been encountered in Chaco and the Guianas.

To establish exact boundaries to the regions where scalping was practiced and where it was not, is impossible, and so likewise as to the period of time. Similar difficulties are also met with in regard to head trophies and allied customs, so that all conclusions are only approximations, caused by the complete lack of records in many cases and an incompleteness of the information in others.

Farrand, in his Basis of American History, says " Scalping was a custom over the whole continent north of Mexico, except at certain points on the Pacific slope and among the Eskimo." The only unconditionally correct part of this statement is that regarding the Eskimo, among whom the habit seems actually to have been wholly unknown. Of the neighbors of the Eskimo, the Athapascan of the north and northwest practiced no scalping, while the Thlinkit did so only in a restricted and not characteristic manner. On Hudson Bay, in Labrador, and toward Newfoundland the Eskimo lived near the Algonquin and Beothuc, of which the former took many an Eskimo scalp, yet the habit was not communicated to the latter. In the eighteenth century the Nottaway, on Moose River, at that time great enemies of the Eskimo, imposed on their dependent Montagnais tribes a yearly tribute of Eskimo scalps.

The Eskimo of Bering Strait took the whole heads of their fallen enemies as trophies, but they learned this custom from the Thlinkit, and were the only branch of the people who practiced it.

Being neither scalpers nor head gatherers, the Eskimo were famed for the mutilations which they practiced on the dead bodies of their enemies. These horrible mutilations were a potent cause of the great hate felt toward the people by all the neighboring Indians. They quartered the bodies, cut or tore them into pieces, abused them, and threw the remains into the water.

The tribes of the Athapascan linguistic family, the neighbors of the Eskimo along a great stretch of the country in the north, also, as a rule and in their old abodes, never scalped. They likewise did not practice head-hunting. In only one of the many reports concerning these tribes has the writer encountered a note that one of them, the Loucheux, took off with them on one occasion as trophies the lower jaws of their fallen enemies. Even the so-called western Athapascan, namely, those who are settled west of the Rocky Mountains on the

Frazer and other rivers, did not generally practice scalping; nevertheless, some of these tribes, probably those that had relations with the more eastern peoples, have adopted the custom. These were the so-called Carriers, the Sicaunies, Talcotin, and Chilcotin. The Athapascan on the Churchill have also learned to scalp from their Algonquin neighbors.

As to the southern tribes speaking the Athapascan and including the Apache, Lipan, Navaho, etc., scalping seems also to have been originally unknown among them, but through contact and mixture (Navaho) with neighboring tribes who practiced the same, after their many wars and after the Mexicans' offers of premiums for scalps, they also adopted the custom to some degree. Ten Kate denied this, and other observers write nothing of scalping on occasions when the Apache would have surely taken the trophies had they cared for them. Even the scalpings reported from Chihuahua and Durango need not have been committed by the Apache, but may have been due to other tribes, parties from which occasionally invaded that territory. Nevertheless, there is the evidence of Gregg, Ruxton, Fröbel, Möllhausen, and Bandelier that scalps were taken by bands of the Apache and also the Lipans. The Navaho, strongly mixed, had a tradition of scalping done by their ancestors. The Hupa in California lived away from the regions of strife with the scalping eastern tribes and remained evidently free from the habit.

All the Athapascan-speaking peoples, and particularly those that lived in the north in the proximity of the Eskimo, mutilated the dead of their enemies.

The whites who came first in contact with the Algonquin found among them two classes of war trophies. The tribes on the lower St. Lawrence, in New Brunswick, Nova Scotia, along the Delaware and Chesapeake bays, down to Carolina, practiced scalping, while the Algonquin who were settled in New England and eastern New York, along the Hudson, did not scalp, but were head-hunters. However, even among the first-named tribes, the custom of scalping was by no means as fully developed and as general as it became later on, and cutting off the entire head and scalping a severed head were also observed. The tribes of the Huron-Iroquois and the Muskhogean linguistic families behaved in a similar manner.

While the Algonquin of the lower St. Lawrence, New Brunswick, Nova Scotia, and northern Maine practiced scalping at the time of the advent of the whites, those farther south, as far as New Jersey, were head-takers only. This peculiarity is explainable by the comparative isolation of the latter between the sea and the mountains on the west, and by their limited intercourse with other tribes speaking the same language. From Chesapeake Bay down to Carolina scalping was again found. These Algonquin were separated from those speaking the same language farther north by tribes speaking Iroquois and who practiced scalping, and the habit was also met with on the lower Delaware.

The great mass of the more western Algonquin became known to the whites much later and the custom of scalping was found among them fully developed. Notwithstanding this the old habit of cutting off the entire head cropped out here and there on favorable occasions; this was particularly the case at the siege of Detroit by the associated tribes under Pontiac. Finally, what has been said of the central Algonquin is also true of their relatives of the plains, the Blackfoot, Cheyenne, and Arapaho.

The Hudson Indians, who originally belonged to the scalping Algonquin, though there is no record that they have ever been observed by the whites to practice the custom, gathered for a time a peculiar kind of a war trophy, namely, the hand. The development of this peculiarity can be traced to the introduction by the Dutch of negro slaves and the reward offered by the owners, according to a widespread habit in Africa, for the right hand of every slave fugitive. The Indians engaged in the pursuit of such fugitives just as the whites did. Later on, when difficulties arose between the whites and some of the natives a reward was set by the former on the hands of the Indians, and in the so-called Esopus war hands of the fallen were cut off and carried away as trophies both by the Hollanders and by the Indians. With, or even before, the end of the Dutch dominion the usage ceased and was eventually replaced by the practice of taking scalps, for which premiums were offered by the English.

The Newfoundland Beothuc exercised, according to Thevet, the custom of scalping in its primitive form.

The Huron-Iroquois were accused of being the probable originators of scalping in North America, but it seems that if there was any single point where the practice was developed and from whence it spread, it must be placed farther south, toward the Gulf of Mexico. It was common at the time of the discovery in Florida, and its spreading thence would also explain its occurrence in the Guianas. The Iroquois may have acquired the custom through the Cherokee, whose legends speak of it as of an old habit, and through the Tuscarora and Susquehannock.

Among the peoples speaking the Timucua and Muskhogee scalping was found by the first whites to be general. In fact, the custom extended all over the territory of the present Gulf States, on both sides of the Mississippi, among the Natchez and Tonika tribes, and farther on to the Caddo of Texas. In the last-named territory a good illustration of the mode of the development of the practice was furnished by the Ceni. On return from one of their war expeditions the warriors brought some scalps, but the women who accompanied them and with whom it was not of such importance to go unencumbered carried whole heads of the enemies.

With the tribes of the Sioux family whites came into contact relatively late, but from all the extant accounts of these tribes it may be safely concluded that scalping was quite common, though of a later development than among the Huron-Iroquois and the Muskhogee. The western Sioux were known up to comparatively recent times to cut off on some occasions the entire heads of the fallen and then scalp them leisurely at the first halting place.

The Osage, according to some Kiowa reports collected by Mooney, are said not to have been scalp hunters; yet we have several very good and detailed accounts of this very people, showing that they did practice scalping in the same manner as all the other Plains tribes, and that they were among those who preserved longest the ceremonies and mourning usages connected with the trophy.

So far as the mounds in the eastern part of North America are concerned, traces of scalping were never discovered. Pieces of animal skin were found in the mounds, but never a scalp, yet all the tribes who were in the habit of taking the scalp lock knew well how to prepare it, and these trophies were often buried with their owner.

The Shoshone and Kiowa scalped to some extent, but here, as elsewhere, the custom received a stimulus through the approach of whites.

So far as the New Mexico and Arizona Pueblo are concerned, there is no mention of scalping in the reports of the first explorers, such as Marcos de Niza, Castañeda, Coronado, or Espejo; but later reports permit the conclusion that scalping was nevertheless quite an old custom among them, though practiced in a primitive and less striking form.

Of the tribes speaking the Piman dialects, some scalped and some did not. Among the former were the Opata and Papago, among the latter the Pima themselves and the Acaxee. Of the Yuma speaking peoples the Mohave, Yuma, and Seri scalped in a primitive manner, while the tribes of the Californian peninsula, though showing certain hair cult, were head and not scalp hunters.

In California, which was occupied by tribes of more than a dozen linguistic families, some of the peoples scalped, others took head trophies, still others eyes or ears, while some took no trophies at all. To give details concerning the many individual tribes is impossible. Neither the scalping nor the head hunting appears to have been practiced intensely or characteristically. So far as the ear trophies are concerned, it is possible that the custom originated in this region. It was practiced extensively in California, Arizona,

New Mexico, and northern Mexico by the Spanish soldiers. The writer has not found that the habit existed anywhere else in North America, except as a punishment for marital infelicity. In one instance it was observed, under special circumstances, among the Aztecs. On the other hand, the ear trophy was very common under Portuguese and Brazilian dominion in South America, and ears were delivered to the authorities by Indians, mixed breeds, and whites. We learn that as late as the first half of the nineteenth century a Brazilian commander brought in 300 ears.

The custom of taking the eyes of the fallen as trophies was also very nearly limited to a part of California, being found in addition only among the Tupi. The eyes were taken out, prepared in a special manner, and preserved in memory of the victory.

Information concerning war customs among the tribes in the Northwest is also not definite. As Lewis and Clark reached the territory of the Shahaptin and Chinook, they were surprised to find for the first time since leaving the Mississippi an absence of scalping and the presence of finger trophies. It seems, however, that the finger trophy custom was not widespread or followed to more than a moderate degree. It was apparently a remnant of a practice that was more widely distributed in the West before the advent of scalping. After the visit of Lewis and Clark, tribes like the Nez Percé, Flathead, Kutenay, and Cayuse carried on scalping.

The cutting off of fingers was found also among other American tribes, some of which lived far apart. It was reported from the Iroquois, Huron, Algonquin, and Tupi, but in most of these cases the object was not to secure a trophy, but rather to mutilate the dead body, partly as a result of hate and partly as a precautionary measure to prevent harm by the spirit of the killed. The severed fingers were especially those used in arrow release. The Araukanian employed fingers cut off from their enemies in their symbolical declaration of war.

Regarding the coast tribes of Washington and northward to the boundaries of the Eskimo, we have many seemingly contradictory statements. Nevertheless by a close study of these it is possible to arrive at some facts.

The warlike Chimakuan tribes were head-hunters, but later on practiced scalping. The Salish, Aht, or Wakash tribes, the Haida, Tsimshian, and Koloshan were all originally head-hunters, but in later times adopted here and there scalping after an intermediary form of procedure. They never practiced scalping to any great extent or in its characteristic form.

In Mexico the farther south we go the more rare the habit of scalp-becomes: its place is occupied by the head trophy.

So much for the distribution of the custom in North America.

8

In South America we find two foci where the habit of scalping prevailed, namely, in northern Argentina, Paraguay, Chaco, and the Guayanas. The method here consisted of decapitation (cutting off the entire head) and then the painstaking removal of the scalp; and in general it underwent no change during several hundred years. The scalp lock was also not as highly prized as among the Indians in North America. It is true that it was an object of pursuit and regard, worn by the women in the scalp dance and flaunted at the enemy before combat; but, besides the scalp, there could be found in the hut of the Chaco Indians also other trophies, such as skulls, calvaria, pieces of skin, prepared beards, etc. Furthermore, the custom did not spread in time to any large extent. The trophy of the majority of the South American tribes was the whole head. The limited extent of the practice of scalping even among the Chaco peoples can probably be attributed to the absence of firearms and steel knives, as well as that of scalp premiums, such as were offered elsewhere by the whites. The absence of firearms was due to strict rules made by the Spanish against their introduction among the natives.

Concerning Guiana, we have the trustworthy statement of Stedman that scalping was practiced by the Carib. As to the Antilles we know but little. Columbus found some heads, in all probabilities trophies, in the dwellings of the aborigines of eastern Cuba. On his second voyage his men found the heads of their comrades, who had been left ashore and were killed by the natives, in the hands of the Haitian. Chanca found skull trophies among the Carib of Guadalupe, and in another place we read of a head in a cooking pot. The boiling of the head served to make its cleaning easier. Besides heads, there were found in the huts of the Carib the whole upper part of the skeleton, flutes made from human bones, and arrow points from the same material. According to all indications, the head was the principal form of trophy all over the Antilles and even in the Guianas.

The negroes of the Guianas and the Maroons in the Antilles brought with them their own forms of trophies. These were first of all prepared right hands, but also heads, with which the negroes played ninepins, and lower jaws, with portions of the scalp, which were used in witchcraft practices. Pinckard reports, however, even true scalping among the Bushmen settled in the Guianas, though no such custom was met there previously by Stedman.

The question arises as to how the occurrence of scalping in the Guianas is to be explained. It was not introduced by the negroes, for, with the exception of its occurrence in the nineteenth century in Dahomey, it was not known on the Dark Continent. The custom was highly developed among the Timucua peoples in Florida, yet the

9

theory that it may have thence been transmitted to Guiana finds
no substantial support.   In a similar way there is no evidence that
it was introduced by the whites.   On the other hand, it does not seem
improbable that it was brought in through the slave trade; that is,
through enslaved Indians brought to Guiana from North America.
Indian slaves from New England, Carolina, Georgia, and Florida
were far dispersed by the whites, and a portion of them were brought
to the mouth of the Orinoco and the shore of South America for
pearl fishing.   It is quite possible that some individuals or parties
from among these Indians, most of whom belonged to scalping
tribes, gained their liberty and, joining some of the natives, introduced the custom of scalping among them.   The source of the practice in Chaco is not traceable.

SPREADING AND DEVELOPMENT OF THE CUSTOM OF SCALPING THROUGH THE INFLUENCE OF EUROPEANS.

It is a well-established fact that the conflicts of primitive peoples,
while very frequent, are in general not attended by many fatalities.
The same was true of the Indians, with the exception of the very
infrequent instances of a success of an attack by surprise, which was
followed by a general massacre.

The introduction of firearms changed this state of affairs.   The
guns became not only the direct cause of a greater number of fatalities, but they also served to demoralize the party armed in a more
primitive manner and facilitated pursuit.   In consequence the wars
became more bloody and there were more scalps.

In North America the natives were supplied with firearms by the
colonists themselves, in some cases surreptitiously, in others openly.
They were also furnished with the iron or steel knife, which greatly
facilitated the removal of the scalp lock.   Formerly the scalping was
done with knives made of various materials.   The reed knife was
found in Brazil, Guiana, and the southeastern part of North America; the shell knife was used along the entire Gulf and north along
the Atlantic coast as far as the territory of the Huron-Iroquois,
also to some extent on the Pacific coast and among the Araukanians;
a fish-tooth knife existed in the Chaco, throughout Brazil and
the Guianas; and a stone knife prevailed in Mexico and neighboring regions, in California, the Rocky Mountains, on the Plains, and
in Texas.   The Apache knew how to sever the scalp lock with the
sinew cord of the bow.   All of these implements possessed disadvan-
tages when compared with the white man's knife, and the latter was
eagerly adopted.   It became a much desired article of commerce and
exchange and was soon used in scalping, upon the frequency and
development of which it must have exerted a stimulating effect.

The "scalping knife," or "scalp knife," had ordinarily the shape of a single-edged butcher knife, but occasionally it was two-edged, like a dirk. The traders usually sold the knife alone, the Indians making the scabbard according to their own liking. The instrument was carried in the belt or on a cord passing about the neck. The prices paid for these knives differed widely. Thus, in 1665 certain Canadian Indians received 8 knives for 1 beaver skin, while in the beginning of the nineteenth century, during the height of the power of the fur companies, $7.50 was paid in their territory for a knife which in England was worth 3½ pence. At about the same period farther south, in the United States, a knife cost $1. Catlin tells us that in 1832 a Sheffield knife, worth perhaps 6 pence, was valued at the price of a horse.

While firearms and steel knives gave a strong impetus to scalping in North America, the acme of the custom was reached after the institution by whites of scalp premiums, accompanied by the employment of the natives by the whites for scalp gathering, and scalping by the whites themselves.

The first to offer premiums for the heads of their native enemies were, in 1637, the Puritans of New England. They asked for the heads, scalping being as yet unknown in that part of the country. As a result, heads of the Pequods were brought in by the colonists and allied Indians in large numbers.

Thirty-eight years after the Pequod war, began that against King Philip, and head premiums were again established. At this period the custom of scalping had already extended into New England, and most of the trophies obtained must have been scalps.

On the 15th of July, 1675, the Connecticut colonists made with one of the Narragansett chiefs a treaty in which they promised for the person of one of the feared Wampanog chiefs 40 cloth coats, or 20 for his head alone, and for each one of his subjects 2 coats if living or 1 if dead. To their own troops they paid 30 shillings for each head. To the "heroine," Hannah Dustin, who with her own hands is said to have taken and brought in the scalps of 2 Indian men, 2 women, and 6 children, the colony paid £50, besides which she received many expressions of thanks and numerous gifts, including a substantial one from Governor Nicholson.

In 1680 scalp prizes were offered by the colonists of South Carolina; in 1689 they offered the high sum of £8 for each scalp of an Indian warrior. About this time we hear for the first time of scalp premiums offered by the French. In 1688 the French Canadians paid for every scalp of their enemies, whether white or Indian, 10 beaver skins, which was also a high price, equivalent in Montreal to the price of a gun with 4 pounds of powder and 40 pounds of lead.

Later on, about 1691, the governor of Canada paid 10 crowns for every scalp, 20 crowns for every white male captive, and 10 crowns for a white female captive. Later on the scalp as well as the captive price was lowered to 1 crown each, though the government officials declared that 10 crowns for the scalp of every existing Iroquois would be a good investment for Louis XIV.

We have seen that it was the English who offered the first scalp premiums, and it was the French who first extended such rewards to the scalps of whites. This latter custom was, however, also adopted before long by the English colonists, and in 1693, but particularly in 1696, premiums were offered explicitly for French scalps. The price per scalp, perhaps on account of the poor Canadian treasury, was always higher among the English than among the French. In 1707, during Queen Anne's war, the English increased the Indian scalp premium for those who were not employed by the government of the colonies to £100.

In 1703, during Queen Anne's war, the young French colony in Louisiana began also to offer scalp rewards, commencing with 10 crowns for each scalp. After this the prices ranged conformably with those in Canada.

In later wars in which the colonists were concerned scalp hunting was incited to still greater intensity. The premiums were large, ranging up to £100 for one scalp; and they applied to Indians as well as to white enemies. The alluring profits and the growing difficulty of securing the trophy led some to skillfully make two or even more scalps out of one, and to other, more grave, abuses; members of friendly tribes and even the white countrymen of the scalpers were not safe, and even graves were made to yield victims. In June, 1755, General Braddock guaranteed his soldiers and Indians £5 for every scalp of the enemy. A reward of $200 was prescribed for the head of the Delaware chief Shingask and £100 for that of the Jesuit Le Loutre. Scalp prices were offered by the State of Pennsylvania. On the 7th of July, 1764, Governor Penn announced the following rewards: For every captured Indian more than 10 years old, $150; for every scalp of a killed Indian, $134; for every captured woman or boy under 10 years of age and belonging to the inimical tribes, $130; and for every scalp of a slain squaw, $50.

The employment by the various colonies of friendly tribes as allies in war fostered scalping. In 1693 Frontenac ceremoniously received from Indians some scalps of the English. In 1746 Governor Clinton received and counted in an open meeting some scalps of Frenchmen, honored with a *nom de guerre* the Indian leader whose band secured them, and then had the Indians perform a war dance before him, in which William Johnson, then the Iroquois agent and later on a baronet and English general, appeared painted and half naked with the Indians. In the French colonies the conditions were similar. Scalping was also practiced during the War of the Revolution, and that on both sides. Serious complaints were made in this regard against the English, and Hamilton, " the hair-buyer general," was on this account for a long time the object of a bitter hatred. There is no doubt that the English, who incited some of the Indians against the colonists, also offered pay for scalps, though this does not seem to have been the subject of any special law or public ruling. English commanders and generals, among others Burgoyne, received scalps in festive gatherings. In the north the English, following Sullivan's expedition, paid $8; in Georgia occasionally £3 for a scalp. So far as the colonies are concerned, among the border population scalping was general, besides which some of the legislatures offered direct premiums. Thus the legislature of South Carolina promised £75 for every scalp of the fighting men of the enemy, £100 for every captured Indian, and £80 for every captured Englishman or negro.

*　　*　　*　　*　　*　　*　　*

In Mexico the first offers of head premiums of which the writer could find a record date from 1616 to 1618, preceding, therefore, by twenty years similar rewards given by the New Englanders during the Pequod war. The occasion for the Mexican offers was the Tepehuane rebellion in the State of Durango. During the eighteenth century, particularly toward its close, and in the beginning of the nineteenth, scalps, which to prevent frauds had to show both ears, seem to have had a definite market value in northern Mexico, but exact data on the subject are wanting. During the second third of the nineteenth century reports concerning scalping are more frequent. In 1835 the legislature of Sonora proclaimed a war of extermination against the Apaches and set the reward of $100 for every Apache scalp. Chihuahua followed in 1837 with an offer of $100 for every scalp of a male, $50 for that of a female, and $25 for that of every Indian child. In 1845 these scalp regulations were also adopted by the other north Mexican States, as a result of which numbers of adventurers formed themselves into scalp-hunting bands. Kirker, the leader of one such, had in the very beginning, through surprising an Indian camp, such success that the treasuries were able to pay him only a part of the scalp money.

In 1848 and succeeding years the conditions became still worse. It was decided in Chihuahua to again employ bands of scalp hunters, and the premiums were advanced to $250 for each captured full-grown Indian or $200 for his scalp; $150 for every captured Indian woman or child under 14 years of age or $100 for each of their scalps, in addition to which the offers carried the right to the spoil. The privilege granted was often abused by the bands, and scalps were taken from other Indians besides the enemies and even from Mexican mestizos, the hair and skin of which can not, in many cases, be distinguished from those of full bloods.

Such a state of affairs lasted for several decades, continuing past the French invasion and well up to the eighties. The rewards offered reached, in 1863 to 1870, the large sums of $200 to $300 for each ordinary scalp and $500 for that of a chief of the Indians.

In Central and South America we find no scalp premiums and no scalp hunting.

The part of the white population most directly concerned in scalping were the frontiersmen, with the hunters, trappers, and miners. Their mode of life and their frequent dealings with the Indians, of friendly as well as unfriendly nature, developed in these men and even women, who were for the most part the descendants of the Scotch-Irish, manners which were not always in accord with those of civilization.   *   *   *

In some cases the Indians and after them the whites severed not only the scalp, but also other hairy parts of the skin or other pieces, and some of these were utilized for tobacco pouches, straps, belts, etc. Such pieces of skin became even, in some instances, articles of trade. In the summer of 1779 the farmers in the neighborhood of Prickets Fort, in West Virginia, killed an Indian who was wounded in a fight, and the body was scalped and skinned. The skin was tanned, and from it were made a saddle, ball bags, and belts. One of the bags is said by Mr. Thwaites to be preserved to this day by a granduncle of one of the farmers who did the skinning. But even the whites were not always safe before other whites in this respect; thus we read in Norton's Redeemed Captive that during the war in 1746 a French youth cut off an arm of a slain New Englander for the purpose of making himself a tobacco pouch.

It is but natural that a custom of such a force and duration as scalping left some permanent traces, which are best recognizable in the language. The word scalp is commonly used as a synonym for the hair-covered skin of the head. It was applied to animals, and one hears to this day about the " scalp " of the puma, bear, wolf, etc. Premiums for wolf scalps were an important item of income and expense among the colonists. In ordinary conversation the term found and to some extent still finds many applications; thus " may I never see a scalp " was a form of oath; and there were the expressions " There can be no scalping between us," " To go a-scalping," "A company of expert hair-dressers," etc. The railroad ticket " scalper " is still a well-known figure. Figuratively, the word was used to denote social conquests, etc.

At the present time scalping in North America has ceased to exist. It has been prohibited, under heavy penalties, by the law, and had to be given up by the conquered Indians with other parts of their former culture. Curiously enough the trophy formerly so common has become a rare article, even in American ethnological museums.

The scalp itself deserves a few special remarks.

To the eastern Indian the scalp lock was the visible proof of personal bravery, the palpable sign of accomplished revenge; it was like his war medal gained honorably from his enemies. However, the trophy did not always remain the property of the individual warrior, for among some of the tribes it was delivered, after the completion of the proper ceremonies and dances, to the chief or the community; yet the one who took the scalp retained always the honor of the deed and the memory of this was manifested on his person by special forms of painting or other decoration. In still other cases the scalp obtained in individual combat with an enemy was the property of the warrior, while those secured after a battle were delivered to the chief or the tribe and were the subject of special disposition.

Among the western Indians the reputation of a man was proportionate to the number of " coups " or strikes which he had accomplished, and the scalp counted simply as a great " coup."

To be worthy of the full honor the warrior was obliged to personally remove the scalp. This accounts for the often reckless efforts made to secure the trophy. This tendency was disadvantageous to the Indians in their fights with whites, for the time required to sever the scalp might have been sufficient to slay several more of the enemy; it was particularly inconvenient during pursuit.

The reasons which occasionally induced a warrior to go on a scalp hunt were especially ambition, a desire to mend a damaged reputation, revenge, conceit or bravado, or eagerness of gain. Even political reasons may have been occasionally the incentive, for the quantity of scalps in a tribe's possession represented a power and would' facilitate the gaining of confederates. With these must be ranged the belief in certain mystic powers identified with the scalp and supposed to be acquired with it, and the necessity of the presence of the trophy at certain ceremonies and burials.

To secure scalps the Indian shunned no distances, obstacles, hunger, or thirst, nor did he shrink even at the prospect of an almost certain death. Journeys up to 1,000 kilometers long were undertaken for the purpose; neither women nor children nor the sick or wounded were spared, and in extreme cases even the dead were disinterred and scalped. On one occasion the Indians allied with the French surprised an English field hospital and scalped all the patients. General

Jackson, not being able even with all the possible precautions to prevent the Creeks from scalping his buried soldiers, adopted the plan of sinking the dead in the river.

To save his own or his friend's scalp the Indian was ready for any sacrifice, for it was with him not simply the matter of a part of his skin, but with it of the soul itself. If it was impossible to save a friend from death at the hands of the enemy and to carry away his body, an endeavor was made to at least take away his scalp into safety. In rare cases only was a member of a tribe scalped by another member of the same for other reasons; Indians executed by their own people were never scalped. In its pure form scalping in the East could only be performed on an enemy, and was an act of national significance, a declaration of war, or a manifestation of the state of war.

The Indians of the West never scalped a suicide, and, according to Major Dodge, they also never scalped a negro; the eastern Indians were in the latter regard, it seems, less particular, for the writer came across two records of the scalping of negroes.

*   *   *   *   *   *   *

The return of the scalp-laden warriors to their community was announced ahead by signal fires or through a special messenger, and the whole population, but particularly the women, prepared for the reception of the party. Such a reception and the following ceremonies were, according to eyewitnesses, most striking and impressive. Among other manifestations, each scalp was greeted by a special characteristic "scalp cry."

The well-prepared scalps served many purposes. They bejeweled their owner, his horse, his tent, his weapons, while scalp or other human hair streamed from the borders of his garments. As signs of a victory they were exhibited in various ways—hung on lines, poles, or fastened to canoes, etc. They played an important rôle in numerous ceremonies, and the scalp dance or ceremony proper was among the most important and widespread of such manifestations. Finally the scalps were buried among his other honors with the warrior.

Though scalping has ceased in North America, yet the scalp dance has not been entirely abandoned. Artificial scalps take the place of the real, but the form of the ceremony is gone through with scrupulous care.

The beliefs as to the consequences of scalping on the soul of the victim differed. Among some tribes it was held that the spirit of the scalped will have no rest in the hereafter; others believed that it was bound to serve to that of the victor, while still others supposed that it was prevented from ever reaching the "happy hunting ground," or that it was wholly annihilated.

16

Fig. No. 37664—Prisoner's Cord—Eames Collection.

30th Annual Archaeological Report, Ministry of Education, Ontario . . . by permission.

Read before the Seventeenth Annual Meeting of the American Association of the History of Medicine, Atlantic City, N. J., May 4-6, 1941.

INDIAN SCALPING

TECHNIQUE IN DIFFERENT TRIBES

GABRIEL NADEAU, M. D.

*Senior Physician, Rutland State Sanatorium,
Rutland, Massachusetts.*

Doctor Archibald in his address following the presentation of the Henry Jacob Bigelow Medal in Boston, in 1937, related how, during the preparation of his address, he had considered discussing the early history of Canadian surgery, until, " happening to make the suggestion at dinner to the family circle, one member of the younger *irreverentsia*, retaining only the phrase " early Canadian surgery," ejaculated, " Ho! scalping, I suppose! "—a remark which gave him pause, he said.[1]

There is more truth than humor in that anecdote; for, if scalping itself cannot be called a surgical operation, the treatment of the scalp wound certainly pertained to surgery. The custom of removing the scalp to secure a trophy or to inflict torture was a new experience not only to the first settlers, of this country as well as of Canada, but also to the surgeons who came with them. Nothing of what the latter had seen in their practice in Europe, in times of war or in times of peace, could remind them of a wound at once so ghastly and so unnecessary. The operation was not fatal in itself and many lived through the ordeal. Sometimes an enemy was scalped alive and sent back to his people; [2] or sometimes a man, fallen on the field of battle and left for dead after being scalped, recovered from the wounds he had received in his body and survived the mutilation he had suffered on his head.

Scalping, as practiced by the Aborigines of this continent, can be described as the forcible removal of the scalp, totally or in part. There were several methods and the technique varied with different tribes and different localities. That fact seems to have escaped the

---

[1] *The New England Journal of Medicine,* 217: 1027, Dec. 23, 1937.

[2] Frederick Webb Hodge (Ed.), *Handbook of American Indians North of Mexico,* (Bull. 30, Bureau of American Ethnology, Washington, D. C., 1906), II, 482.

178

Fig. 1.

The first graphic representation of scalping. (Courtesy of Argosy Book Stores, New York.) shows the warriors of Outina, a Cacique of the Timucuans of Florida, scalping their enemies. is by Jacques Le Moyne, surnamed de Morgues, an artist who came to Florida with the uguenots under René de Laudonnière, in 1563. Le Moyne escaped the massacre by the paniards at Fort Caroline and went to England where he died. After his death, his manuscripts d drawings were sold by his widow to De Bry, by whom they were first published under e title of *Brevis Narratio Eorum Quae in Florida, Americae Provincia Gallis Acciderunt, cunda in allam Navigatione, duce Renato de Laudonniere, classis Praefecto. Anno MDLXIII.* rankfort, 1591.) The picture shows, on the left, the taking of the trophies; on the right, eir " processing " and, in the background, the carrying away of the trophies to the village. also shows the particular way of " signing off " of the Timucuans : with arrow in ano.

179

19

notice of those who have written on the warfare customs of the Indians. The purpose of this article is to describe those methods briefly.

Scalping first differed in the amount of skin taken from the head. If all the scalp was removed, it was *total*; if only a portion of it, it was *partial*. It also differed in the number of scalps lifted from the same head. If only one scalp was taken, it was *single*; of more than one, it was *multiple*. If the removal of the scalp from the cranium was not preceded by a circular incision through the skin, scalping was then called by *sabrage* or by a saber-like blow. And there was also the scalping of those who were bald-headed or wore their hair cut close. The scalp, in those cases, was wrenched away *with the teeth*. Finally, scalping could be *complete* or *incomplete*. If the flap of skin was left hanging in the back of the neck by a pedicle, it was incomplete. Otherwise, it was complete.

Total Scalping.

Scalping which I call total was of two kinds. One was *simple*; and, in this kind, all of the scalp, but only the scalp, was lifted. The other was *compound*; that is to say, certain parts of the face or neck, besides the scalp, were removed from the head.

a. Total Simple Scalping.

Certain tribes, those especially who lived in the East, removed only the scalp from the head, but removed it in its entirety. I take the following description of that form of scalping from an author who wrote towards the end of the seventeenth century: " When those Indians have killed a man," wrote he, " they always carry away with them, as a trophy, the proof of his death. That trophy is, in their opinion, a visible sign of their courage and bravery; it is the human scalp. They remove it as nicely as one would the skin of a rabbit. First they cut the skin to the bone all around the head with a knife. They start in front, in the middle of the forehead, follow around and behind one ear, then in back of the neck and around the other ear and finish in front where they started. Then after pulling a little on the hair to raise the edge of the skin, they throw the head

Fig. 2.

"An Indian Warrior Entering His Wigwam with a Scalp."
(Thomas Anburey, *Travels through the Interior Parts of America*,
London, 1791. Courtesy of Mr. Clifford K. Shipton, Librarian
of the American Antiquarian Society, Worcester, Mass.) The
artist who made this picture never saw an Indian and probably
copied Le Moyne de Morgues. The scalping instrument was not
the axe, but the sheathed knife hanging on the chest.

181

backward on their knees, and peel off the scalp as easily as one would a glove from the hand." [3]

b. *Total Compound Scalping.*

Some tribes were in the habit of denuding the heads of their enemies more radically. Sometimes they pulled the ears off with the scalp; sometimes, the eyes. Sometimes the whole skin of the face came off, or a portion of the skin of the back. The Chinooks, a tribe of the Pacific coast, for instance, practiced scalping in the following manner: " Those Indians," wrote Duflot de Mofras, " use either a knife or a sharp bone to scalp their enemies. They make an incision above the forehead, over the ears, and down along the neck, as far as the shoulder blades. Then, getting hold of the flap of skin in the back, they pull the whole scalp off while they keep their victim immobilized on the ground with their feet on his shoulder." [4]

The Sioux, a tribal group who inhabited the great Plains, sometimes removed the ears with the scalp. The knife, instead of passing over the ears, simply passed under them and they came off with the skin of the head. The Indian who wore ear ornaments, like rings and pendants of haliotis or metal, was sure to lose his ears with his scalp if he fell in battle; because adornment gave added value to his scalp. " In former years," wrote Clark, " the Sioux Indians, if they had time, cut off the heads of their slain enemies and took them to their first camp after the fight, where the entire scalp was taken off. To make it particularly fine, they kept on the ears with the rings and ornaments." [5]

Scalping of the Vertex or Partial Scalping.

Certain tribes, those who inhabited the Plains, for instance, and others, preferred to carry off only a small portion of the scalp. That portion, located over the vertex, was a " small circular patch of skin

[3] Cyprien Tanguay, *A travers les régistres* (Montreal, 1886), 94.

[4] *Exploration du Territoire de l'Orégon, des Californies et de la mer Vermeille, exécutée pendant les années 1840, 1841 et 1842.* (Paris, 1844), II, 356.

[5] W. P. Clark, *The Indian Sign Language, with Brief Explanatory Notes of the Gestures Taught Deaf-Mutes in our Institutions for Their Instruction and a Description of Some of the Peculiar Laws, Customs, Myths, Superstitions, Ways of Living, Code of Peace and War Signals of our Aborigines* (Philadelphia, 1885), 326.

at the root of the scalplock just back of the crown of the head," or over it.[6] "That scalp" wrote Catlin, " is procured by cutting out a piece of the skin of the head, the size of the palm of the hand or less, containing the very center or crown of the head, the place where the hair radiates from a point, and exactly over what the phrenologists

Fig. 3.

Four different forms of scalping. (Bressany, *Relation abrégée de quelques missions* . . . , Montréal, 1852.) On the left, a total simple scalping. In the center, a partial and a multiple scalping. The vertex has already been lifted by one Indian; while another is coming to remove a second scalp from the fallen man's head. On the right, a scalping by *sabrage*.

call self-esteem."[7] It is done, he said, " by grasping the left hand into the hair on the crown of the head, and passing the knife around it through the skin, tearing off a piece of the skin with the hair. (. . .) To be a genuine scalp, [it] must contain and show the crown or centre of the head."[8]

[6] Frederick Webb Hodge, *Op. cit.*, II, 482.
[7] George Catlin, *Letters and Notes on the Manners, Customs, and Condition of the North American Indians* (Philadelphia, 1857), I, 60.
[8] Catlin, *Op. cit.*, I, 362.

The custom of those tribes was to mark off on their heads the region to be scalped. It was a sort of defiance and an incitement to their enemies to come and scalp them.[9] The hair was cut close to the head except for a lock on the top which was called the *scalplock*. The scalplock was generally hung with ornaments or finely plaited and sometimes a circle of ochre or vermilion was painted around it. " The majority of the Plains Indians," wrote Clark, " braid that portion of the hair contained in a circle, about two inches in diameter, at the crown of the head. The braid is formed of three strands, and the circle is marked by pulling out the hair, and this little circular path is painted, usually with red ochre. The hair of the head is parted in the middle, and the parting extends to this circle. The scalplock seems meant to be a mark of manhood and defiance, a sort of " take it if you dare and can " idea. It is marked out and braided when a boy reaches the age of about five years, and covers the space called the crown or curl of the hair, so that anyone can readily tell when he sees a scalp whether it is genuine ; *i. e.,* only from this portion of the head." [10]

I am reminded here of a story of a French murderer who had been sentenced to die on the guillotine. When he was prepared for execution, a dotted line was found tattooed on his neck, with, a little below, the words : " Please cut on the dotted line."

To the man who had not been felled by a mortal blow, it made a great deal of difference whether the whole of his head or only a portion of it had been denuded. The removal of all the scalp left a large, messy wound ; while the scalping of the vertex inflicted only a minor injury. " Usually the scalps taken [by the tribes of the Prairies] were small," wrote Grinnell, " a little larger than a silver dollar." [11] It is obvious that a wound of that size was less serious

---

[9] Rev. Peter Jones, *History of the Ojebway Indians* . . . (London, 1861), 76.

[10] Clark, *Op. cit.,* 328. On the question of scalping in general, one may consult Georg Friederici's *Skalpieren und Ähnliche Kriegsgebräuche in Amerika* (Braunschweig, 1906). That work, published in Germany, is very scarce in this country. I know of only one copy of it. It is in the Library of Congress. The Smithsonian Institution published in its *Annual Report* for 1906 a good résumé of Friederici's thesis.

[11] George Bird Grinnell, Coup and Scalp among the Plains Indians, *American Anthropologist* (Lancaster, Pa.). N. S., 12 : 304, 1910. " But like any other piece of fresh skin they stretched greately," when they were mounted on hoops.

Fig. 4.

The three operations of scalping done with one hand. (George Catlin, *Letters and Notes on the Manners . . . of the North American Indians,* Philadelphia, 1857.) The Indian holds up the child with one hand while, with the other, he (a) has already incised the skin around the head with his knife, (b) is now prying off the edge of the scalp from the cranium with the tip of his thumb and (c) will finish the mutilation by grasping the skin to strip it off. The rest of the family is resignedly awaiting their fate.

185

and required less care and attention than a wound that involved the whole surface of the hairy skin of the head.

The usual complications which followed the avulsion of the scalp were bleeding, infection and necrosis of the bony structure underneath. In scalping of the vertex, bleeding was inconsiderable, of short duration and easily stopped; while, in total scalping, the loss of blood was considerable and very difficult to control. As to the danger of infection, it was obviously greater with a large wound than with a small one. The infection was generally localized to the skin and the neighboring tissues. But sometimes it became generalized and the patient died of septicaemia or meningitis. Necrosis of the cranium, or caries, was a long delayed complication and did not usually manifest itself until a few years after the initial injury. The outer table, being deprived of its blood supply, became dry and black, and after a while, rotted away. The necrotic process continued and reached the inner table and soon a foramen appeared through which issued the substance of the brain. There was less chance of necrosis in partial scalping than in more extensive denudation, because the bone was not uncovered for any considerable extent and the supply of blood to the outer table was never much affected by the stripping off of the epicranium.

Multiple Scalping.

Scalping was called multiple when several warriors, each one in his turn, removed a portion of a man's scalp from his head. Every one of the pieces taken counted for a whole scalp and had the value of a trophy. That custom owed its origin to the difficulty which arose sometimes, after a battle, of agreeing upon the real victor. To settle arguments which often degenerated into fights, it was decided that, when several warriors had taken part in striking a man down, his scalp would be divided amicably and each would take a piece of it. The piece was taken directly from the head, however, and not cut from the scalp after the latter had been removed from the cranium. The choice piece, that is, the portion covering the crown or vertex, was left to the chief, or to the man who had struck first, or to the one who had inflicted the most serious wound, when that fact could be determined by the contestants.

The habit of taking several scalps from the same head became more frequent after the introduction of firearms. The reason for it is obvious. The wounds caused by bullets were anonymous, so to speak; while those inflicted by arrows could be more easily identified.

Fig. 5.

Avulsion of the scalp by the hair followed by the Death-Cry and the Elevation of the trophy. (Catlin, *op. cit.*) Long hair permitted a quicker denudation and gave more value to the trophy.

Scalping by Sabrage.

Scalping consists of two operations separate and distinct. First, a circular incision with a sharp instrument which isolates a segment of the scalp from the rest of the skin. Then the avulsion of that segment from the cranium. Sometimes, however, time did not permit such an uncomplicated and simple procedure and the preliminary incision was dispensed with.

The head was seized by the hair and a quick, strong pull was made which loosened the skin from the bone over a certain area. Then the knife, like a saber, as a sickle, swooped down and cut off a portion of the scalp. That method, the saber-like blow, or *sabrage* method never allowed more than a relatively small area of skin to be lifted and always brought on injury to the outer table of the skull, by removing portions of the periosteum. A slow necrosis followed and, after a while, the bone crumbled away and the substance of the brain became exposed. "As soon as the man has fallen," wrote Pouchot, "they run to him, put their knee between his shoulders, take a lock of hair in one hand, and with their knife in the other give a blow separating the skin from the head, and tearing off a piece." [12]

Sometimes, more than one blow was necessary. "They seize the head of the disabled or dead enemy," wrote Carver, "and placing one of their feet on the neck, twist their left hand in the hair; by this means, having extended the skin, that covers the top of the head, they draw out their scalping knives, which are always kept in good order for this purpose, and with a few dexterous strokes take off the part that is termed the scalp." [13]

Avulsion with the Teeth

After the skin had been incised around the head, it was necessary to raise the edge of the scalp a little so that the fingers could seize it and pull it off. A jerk on the hair was usually enough to accomplish that. The hair then served not only to immobilize the head during the incision but also to pull off the scalp afterward. But what if the man was bald or if his head had been shaved? The scalp was then removed with the teeth.

---

[12] Pierre Pouchot, *Memoir upon the Late War in North America* . . . (Transl. by Franklin B. Hough, Roxbury, Mass., 1866), II, 246.

[13] Jonathan Carvar, *Three Years' Travels throughout the Interior Parts of North America* . . . (Charlestown, 1802), 188-189.

Fig. 6.

Avulsion by the skin. (De Bonnechose, *Montcalm et le Canada Français,* Paris, 1886.) When the hair was too short, the denudation was done by grasping the scalp with the hand and pulling it off. The Death-Cry and the Elevation, or Presentation, of the trophy immediately followed the removal of the scalp.

189

a. *Cropped Hair.*

Many tribes cut their hair close to the head, leaving sometimes only a ridge from the forehead to the crown, " where the scalplock was parted off in a circle, stiffened with fat and paint, made to stand erect, and curved like a horn." [14] " If the hair is short," wrote Anburey, " and they have no purchase with their hand, they stoop, and with their teeth strip it off." [15]

It seems that certain tribes always used their teeth to peel off the cranium after the incision had been made with the knife. Here is how Dr. James Thacher described scalping as peformed by the tribes who lived along the Hudson at the time of the Revolution: " With a knife they make a circular cut from the forehead quite round, just above the ears, then taking hold of the skin with their teeth, they tear off the whole hairy scalp in an instant, with wonderful dexterity." [16]

Among certain tribes the chiefs were in the habit of cutting all their hair very close, without leaving a scalplock on the top of their heads or a ridge in the middle. The following is an abstract from the Journal of a French officer: " July 30, 1757. A party of 13 friendly Mohawks arrived at the camp. They bring with them four scalps which they took near Schamaken. They told me that they thought they had killed a chief, because one of the scalps is only a shaved piece of skin." [17]

b. *Bald Heads.*

Baldness, in any form, is very uncommon in Indians; and the first bald heads beheld by the Red Man belonged to Europeans.[18] But, by what I have just said about the scalping of those who wore

---

[14] Hodge, *Op. cit.,* I, 524.

[15] [Thomas Anburey], *Travels through the Interior Parts of America* (London, 1791), I, 354. The " war dance " was a representation of the different manoeuvres of discovering, attacking and scalping an enemy.

[16] James Thacher, *A Military Journal during the American Revolutionary War* . . . (Boston, 1827), 114.

[17] Relations et Journaux, *Collections des Manuscrits du Maréchal de Lévis* (Quebec, 1895), 113.

[18] Aleš Hrdlička, *Physiological and Medical Observations among the Indians* . . . , 161-162 (Bull. 34, Bureau of American Ethnology, Washington, 1908).

their hair cut close, it will be seen that the scalping of bald heads presented no problem at all. First a circle was traced with a knife on the bald pate, then the skin was wrenched away with the teeth. Ross Cox tells of the scalping of an old man, ninety-two years old, who had only a few hairs left on his head. " His body was found by the Flatheads, close to a beaver dam :—a ball had penetrated his temples,

Fig. 7.

The Scalp Dance. (Catlin, *op. cit.*)

and the few white hairs that remained on his aged head did not prevent his inhuman butchers from stripping it of the scalp." [19]

I should like to relate here an anecdote concerning the Count de Frontenac who was Governor General of Canada during the French regime. It seems that the Count was bald, but his baldness was well concealed by the ornamented peruke which he wore in common with all the noblemen of that period. He was on an expedition against the Iroquois. One day, as he was crossing a river with his army in full

[19] Ross Cox, *Adventures on the Columbia River* (New York, 1832), 172. That man was a Frenchman who had fought at the battle on Abraham's Plains. He was supposed to have "assisted in carrying the Marquis de Montcalm into Quebec, after he had received his death-wound."

view of the enemies who were standing on the opposite bank, he jumped into the river, removed his wig quickly while under the water and came up with not a hair, true or false, on his head. These Indians had never seen a bald man and they were stunned. They declared immediately that the Governor had scalped himself. And a man, red or white, according to their code of war, who scalped himself could only be a man who was desperate and willing to win at all costs or die. They all fled in terror and left the field to Frontenac.[20]

That story, most probably, is not authentic. Bossu, in his *Travels through Louisiana,* relates one that is almost similar. A certain Mr. du Tissenet was travelling with some Indians whose language he understood. Unaware of that, they were plotting among themselves, under his nose, how to kill him. He wore his hair very short and had it covered with a peruke which his companions mistook for his natural hair. As they were remarking to one another how beautiful his hair was and how nice it would be to scalp him, du Tissenet, all of a sudden, seized his peruke and threw it at their feet, exclaiming at the same time: "You want my scalp, you treacherous scoundrels? Here it is. Take it." They were too terrified to say a word. They ran away and du Tissenet was able to escape with his life.[21]

Incomplete Scalping

The different types of scalping which I have described so far are all *complete* scalpings; that is, they are scalpings in which there was complete separation of the scalp from the cranium. That form was the most common form of scalping practiced by the Indians.

There was, however, a type of scalping, called *incomplete,* in which the avulsion was not finished. The scalp was left hanging in back in the neck by a small pedicle. That form of mutilation was not common and was performed by certain tribes only during torture and burning at the stake. "When everything is ready," says a *Relation* of 1666, "the prisoner is brought out and tied to the stake and finally burnt. When he is burnt up to the stomach, they detach

---

[20] Jean-Baptiste d'Aleyrac, *Aventures militaires au XVIII° siècle* (Paris, 1935), 41.

[21] Bossu, *Nouveaux Voyages aux Indes* . . . (Amsterdam, 1769), I, 176-177.

him, break all his fingers, raise the scalp which was left hanging behind by a small tongue of skin to the head. They put him to death in these agonies, after which each takes his morsel and proceeds to make merry." [22] Certain tribes were in the habit oi inflicting torture by pouring burning sand or boiling gum over the denuded cranium. It is possible that the purpose of leaving the scalp hanging was to

Fig. 8.

Hunter scalped by Indians near Fort Dodge, Kansas, in 1869, and photographed by the Frontier Photographer, William H. Jackson. Probably the only photograph in existence of a man scalped by the Indians. (*The Oregon Trail*. Courtesy of the Federal Writers Project and the Smithsonian Institution.)

keep the sand or the gum in place on the head by throwing the skin back over it. The incomplete scalping might also have had some other significance, ceremonial or symbolical, which has so far remained unexplained.

[22] The Nine Iroquois Tribes, 1666, *Documents Relative to the Colonial History of the State of New York* (Edmund Bailey O'Callaghan, Ed., Albany, 1855), IX, 49.

Conclusion

My purpose is to describe the major forms of scalping as practiced by the North American Indians. The minor varieties I have not deemed of sufficient interest to warrant description here. I have also omitted any mention of scalping by the White Man. The Europeans learned to scalp from the Indians and some of them, traders, interpreters, voyageurs, became very adept pupils. I should like to end this article with two cases of scalping by Whites. First, a Frenchman from Louisiana: " The Indian fell at the blow and the Frenchman on him; the next moment, the latter was up, and shouting the death cry, scalped his enemy, and came in triumph to present the trophy to the general, who in return ordered some goods to be delivered to him." [23] And now an Englishman: " While Goddin was smoking in his turn, Bird gave a sign to the Indians, and a volley was fired in his back. While he was yet living, Bird himself tore the scalp from the poor fellow's head and deliberately cut Captain Wyeth's initials, N. J. W., in large letters upon his forehead." [24]

The work of this Englishman, nobody will deny it, had a quality of craftsmanship that was sadly lacking in that of the Frenchman.

[23] History of Louisiana, Translated from the Historical Memoirs of M. Dumont, *Historical Collections of Louisiana* (B. F. French, Ed., New York, 1853), V, 54.

[24] Townsend's Narrative of a Journey Across the Rocky Mountains, 1834, Reuben Gold Thwaites, *Early Western Travels*, XXI, 354.

THE TORTURE OF CAPTIVES BY THE INDIANS OF EASTERN NORTH AMERICA

NATHANIEL KNOWLES

University of Pennsylvania

(Communicated by Clark Wissler)

ABSTRACT

The Indians of eastern North America evinced great emotional satisfactions from the prolonged tortures often inflicted upon war captives. Such behavior must be evaluated in terms of the motivations imposed by the various cultures of the several tribes, particularly with respect to the social and religious connotations of the war patterns. This analysis suggests that many groups tortured primarily in retaliation against the whites, who had immediately introduced the common European practise of burning at the stake, and against the Iroquois. Both along the lower Mississippi River and among the Iroquois torture seems to have had strong religious significance with the concept of human sacrifice underlying the act. However the complexes were otherwise so markedly unlike that direct diffusion between the Iroquois and lower Mississippi River groups is not indicated. Both had definite, but different, parallels with sacrifice in Middle America which may indicate a distant common origin for them.

INTRODUCTION

SATISFACTIONS derived through the infliction of physical pain upon a human being are of great psychological significance. In our own culture pleasure arising from the suffering of another is not socially acceptable. When it is experienced, it must be disguised, and even though openly manifest must be rationalized. Torturing, literally twisting, was ingeniously developed at least as early as Greek and Roman times, and perhaps reached its height during the Inquisition of the Middle Ages. The practice had obvious utilitarian motives. As a punishment for certain crimes, torture probably acted as a strong influence for the preservation of order. Of possibly more importance, first to the State and later to the Church, was the information obtained on treason and heresy, from those subjected to it. In addition, the necessity for confession, and hence the ultimate salvation of the soul of the victim, was one of the rationalizations of the Inquisition. Elaborate legal regulations were considered necessary so that the infliction of torture would be purposeful and not merely represent individual brutality. Nevertheless, personal satisfactions, not only to the actual torturers but also vicariously to much of the population, were undoubtedly present although culturally condemned.

Many American Indian tribes did not so inhibit the enjoyment of physical suffering, and the pleasure of whole groups of people was apparently unrestrained during the long tortures inflicted upon a captive.   However, it must be realized that overt manifestations of behavior can be properly evaluated only after an understanding of the underlying motivations, which implies a detailed functional and historical analysis of the culture.   Not until the integration of torture in the culture as a whole is known can the factors affecting individual acts of cruelty be appreciated.   The psychological significance of pleasure derived from the sufferings of another is not within the scope of this study, which is to determine, as far as the available material permits, the integration of torture in the cultures under consideration and the significance to the individual implied by such relationships.

There were two specific, material trophies of a successful war party recognized by the eastern Indians.   These were scalps and captives.   Attainment of honors through the coup as practised by the Plains Indians was entirely unknown.   Important as these trophies were, their value did not outweigh the loss of a man, and a leader who failed to bring back his party intact was condemned as unsuccessful.   Plunder was of little significance as a motive for war since all the tribes were approximately at the same level of material culture.   Naturally, after white contact, knives, guns and other European goods of great value to the Indians were taken as booty.   The horse was of slight importance in the woodlands and did not become an object of raids such as occurred on the plains of the west.   Territorial aggrandizement per se does not seem to have been a cause of war, but rather to have resulted from tribal movements originating from other motives.   The region was rich in natural resources such as game, fish and edible plants, and agriculture was practised, yet the population was sparse.   Consequently, there would have been little economic reason for the usurpation of lands.   White interference changed the original war pattern greatly, as all the tribes were brought into the Spanish, French and English race for empire.   Trade relations for goods, slaves and scalps were established, and it became advantageous for the Indian to side with one or the other of the European nations and to fight for his benefactor with the European weapons which were provided.

Supernatural elements were intimately associated with the war complex over the entire region. Purificatory rites were usually required both before and after war, and there were many strict prohibitions while actually on the war-path. Sexual continence on the part of the warriors might be demanded during the entire period of hostilities. A sacred bundle might be carried to war by the leader, or the warriors might have individual talismen for supernatural protection and assistance. Communications from the supernatural world through the medium of omens or dreams were carefully noted and acted upon, even to the extent of forcing a return from the war-path after days of travel. Failure would usually be attributed to lack of purity on the part of the leader or some other member of the party. Scalps and captives often had significance either in connection with mourning and the appeasement of ghosts, or as offerings to the supernatural. In general, success in war meant the satisfaction of supernatural compulsives which in turn led to social recognition, and was about the only way such recognition could be obtained.

While scalps and captives were the basis of the war trophy pattern of all the tribes within the region, distinctly different attitudes towards these trophies may be discerned. Therefore, torture, which was primarily one method of disposal of one kind of trophy, that is captives, can be evaluated properly only in terms of the more inclusive war trophy complex.

Historical considerations are obviously pertinent to a full understanding of cultural phenomena, and especially so with respect to traits associated with warfare, an activity implying group contacts and often involving the assimilation of captives. History reconstructed from a comparative analysis of cultures at a specific point of time is merely suggestive, and must be used cautiously to supplement conclusions based upon internal evidence. This is particularly true where only small segments of the total culture are under consideration, as in this paper. However, it is hoped that detailed studies of enough more material will eventually be forthcoming so that evidence which can now be treated as no more than historical possibility will be confirmed, thereby further clarifying the specific behavior patterns under discussion here.

The utilization of actual historical records is an entirely different matter. In so far as these either contain descriptions of torturing or fail to mention it at all, they are important and have been discussed at some length.

The accounts contained in the Spanish, French, English and American records of exploration, colonization, trading and missionary activity in the Southeast are almost the sole sources of information. By the first half of the nineteenth century the aboriginal population had been thoroughly defeated and the remnants removed to reservations. Consequently, there are no full accounts of any of the cultures by competent ethnologists, except in so far as traits survived almost inextricably mixed with white and negro elements. The entire war complex, including torturing, obviously would remain as nothing more than a vague tradition. Although the early records of untrained observers cannot be expected to furnish fully satisfactory accounts of cultural details, nevertheless some are reasonably full and often surprisingly acute. Religious beliefs, social organization and ceremonial procedures are poorly described, but on the other hand the torture of captives is a trait which would seem to be particularly subject to casual observation, at least in its main outlines. The conflict between the invading whites and the "barbarians" was of constant concern to the missionaries, colonists and traders. The brutalities practised upon anyone so luckless as to fall into their hands were an ever present threat. We might well expect an overdrawn picture of Indian cruelties to serve as an excuse to wipe out these "savages" who resisted the depredations of the whites, and in general this may well be true. On the contrary, understatements of the dangers would be unusual except possibly in a few cases of colonization propaganda.

Additional sources may be tapped although it is unlikely that further data of particular significance will be forthcoming. Archæological evidence may possibly be uncovered which will throw some light on the subject of torture, but it should be realized that too much cannot be expected. Little can be deduced from charred bones and burnt stakes which will permit the reconstruction of torture or human sacrifice. Scalps have not been found in the mounds, and it is unlikely that they will be uncovered. Most of the material associated with the war complex was of a perishable nature, thus precluding the possibility of archæological evidence.

The infliction of pain upon another person may not be confined solely to the treatment of war captives, and other such acts may have a bearing upon any final psychological interpretation of torture. However, it has been thought desirable to limit this paper to the torture of war captives. Such behavior as individual brutality to wife, child or other person, institutionalized punishment for adultery or other crimes, infliction of pain in ceremonies such as initiation rites, and self-torture of the Plains Sun Dance type, are not of immediate concern.

The specific region under consideration is that commonly known as the Southeastern Culture Area of North America. This may be defined geographically as lying east of the Mississippi River and south of the northern parts of Virginia and Kentucky. In addition, the southern Caddoans of Louisiana and eastern Texas and the Iroquois of Pennsylvania and New York have been included. Material pertaining to the adjacent groups, such as the Algonkians, the Plains Area and Middle America, will be used only in so far as it contributes to the clarification of the problem. The material has thus been limited to a geographically contiguous area within which actual contacts of all the groups can be predicated and the uncertainties inherent in spatially discontinuous distributions eliminated. The various manifestations of torture have been correlated, as far as the data permit, with other phases of the war complex and the sacrifice of human life. Not only is an essentially continuous distribution of torture involved, but it seems to have been absent in adjacent regions except where it had penetrated in relatively recent times as a retaliation against enemies who used it.

Unfortunately the material is extremely scanty for many tribes, and for others which would normally be included, such as the Atakapa and Chitimacha, the insufficiency of data has compelled their exclusion from consideration.

I. Descriptive Material on Torture

Detailed descriptions of the tortures inflicted by the Indians of Southeastern North America are relatively rare; in most cases their acts are merely referred to as cruel or horrible without any indication whether or not prolonged tortures rather than either brutal slaying or mutilation of the dead were involved. In striking contrast to this situation is the abundance of detailed accounts of the prolonged agonies inflicted by the Northern Iroquois upon their enemies.

The following descriptions, arranged in approximately chronological order, include any behavior towards captives which might indicate that torturing was involved. As the absence of the practise at a particular time and place is also pertinent to an understanding of the torture complex in the region, data which indicate that it was lacking have been included.

The first unquestioned landing of the Europeans upon the mainland of the New World was the expedition of Ponce de Leon [1] which first touched Florida in the neighborhood of the present St. Augustine [2] and then coasted southward without attempting to make land again owing to the hostility of the natives. While off the southwest tip of the Florida peninsula Ponce de Leon was addressed in Spanish by an Indian,[3] thus making it apparent that the atrocious cruelty of the Spanish for some twenty years in the West Indies had become known to the inhabitants of the mainland prior to the discovery of the continent by the whites. Their determined resistance and lack of superstitious fear of the white man indicated, according to Lowery, an appreciation of the treatment to be expected.[4]

During the succeeding years numerous expeditions such as those of Miruelo and Cordova which were driven off by the Indians,[5] Alvarez de Pineda which remained some forty days at a large town at the mouth of a great river,[6] Gomez,[7] Verazzani,[8]

---

[1] The records are not clear as to the extent of prior explorations, including those of the Cabots and Americus Vespucci. For a discussion of the whole problem see Lowery, 1911, especially pp. 124, 127, 130 and Winsor, II, p. 232.

[2] Fairbanks, p. 16.

[3] Lowery, 1911, p. 142.

[4] Lowery, 1911, p. 144.

[5] Lowery, 1911, p. 149.

[6] Mississippi, Lowery, 1911, p. 150—Mobile Bay, Swanton, Southeastern Indians, p. 5.

[7] Lowery, 1911, p. 169.

[8] Verarzanus, John, Relation of.

and most likely other unauthorized and therefore unrecorded explorations were in all probability largely in the nature of slave raids.[9] Scant information on the aboriginies is found in any of these accounts but they do emphasize the possible extent of Spanish cruelty. The treatment accorded the inhabitants [10] is perhaps typified by the following action of an expedition sent out by Ayllon in 1519:

> Although Ayllon had charged Gordillo to cultivate friendly relations with the Indians of any new land he might discover, Gordillo joined with Quexos in seizing some seventy of the natives, with whom they sailed away. . . .[11]

An account of the Indians [12] met by a later Ayllon expedition to the east coast obtained from a captive does not specifically refer to torture but the following description is perhaps indicative of its absence:

> The inhabitants of this country do not eat human flesh; the prisoners of war are enslaved by the victors.[13]

Much of what later was assumed to be first contact with the Indians had unquestionably been preceded by marauding expeditions which would account for the immediate hostility towards later colonizers.[14]

With Cabeza de Vaca's account of the Narvaez expedition of 1527 we begin to find more solid ethnographic fact. Narvaez and his 600 colonists and soldiers probably landed just west of Tampa Bay.[15] Probably many unknown Spaniards survived the destruction of this expedition and lived for many years among the Indians. The effect of such residence, as well as the journey of the four men to the Pacific Coast, must have had definite repercussions on the aboriginal cultures. Vaca, who has furnished some excellent ethnographic material on the tribes he encountered, fails to mention torture, although he refers to

---

[9] Lowery, 1911, p. 171, suggests that many such unrecorded raids as far north as Chesapeake Bay in quest of slaves may have occurred.

[10] Identified as Cusabo by Swanton, *Early History*, p. 131.

[11] Winsor, II, p. 239. Also see Martyr, II, p. 256.

[12] Identified as Siouans by Swanton, *Early History*, p. 42.

[13] Martyr, II, p. 261.

[14] Mooney's conclusion probably typifies the situation along the entire coast: "Jamestown Colonists landed among a people who already knew and hated the whites." *Powhatan Confederacy*, p. 129.

[15] For a discussion of this location see Lowery, 1911, pp. 453–455.

Indian slayings of Spaniards and of other Indians, and makes observations on war practices.[16]

John Ortis, a member of the Narvaez expedition, was found twelve years later by De Soto soon after he landed in Florida. From him comes probably the earliest account of the treatment of a captive by the Indians of the New World, in this case Timucuans:[17]

Ucita commanded to bind John Ortis hand and foot upon four stakes aloft upon a raft, and to make a fire under him, that there he might be burned.[18]

Almost an identical account is given by Garcilaso de la Vega:

. . . cacique, who, enraged that Ortis could endure so many divers hardships, ordered, on a day of entertainment, that they should kindle a fire in the middle of the public square, that they should put a griddle upon the fire; and that they should put his slave upon it, in order to burn him alive.[19]

Neither Biedma, Ranjel, nor De Soto refer to this incident although they all speak of finding Ortis. He was saved through the intervention of the wife and daughter of the Chief.

Three companions had been seized with Ortis but had not survived the initial abuse:

Harriga guarded with care his prisoners, in order to increase by their death the pleasures of a feast which he was to celebrate, in a few days, according to the custom of the country. The time of the ceremonies arrived, he commanded that the Spaniards, entirely naked, should be compelled to run by turns from one extremity of the public square to the other, that at times arrows should be shot at them, in order that their death might be the slower, their pain the more exquisite, and the rejoicing more noted and of longer duration.[20]

Apart from the above there is no mention of Indian torture in any of the De Soto chronicles.[21] This is quite amazing for if torture in any form had been practised there is every reason to assume that it would have been noted and commented upon by the Spaniards. Swanton in discussing this striking omission writes:

[16] Bandelier, Ad. f., *The Journey of Alvar Munez Cabeza de Vaca.*
[17] According to Swanton, *Early History*, p. 379.
[18] Elvas, p. 125.
[19] Vega, pp. 259–260.
[20] Vega, p. 259.
[21] The Indians of Alabama mimicked throwing a man into the fire. As they first hit him on the head, it does not resemble torture, Elvas, p. 165.

. . . I am inclined to think it indicates that much of this cruelty was of later introduction.[22]

Although accounts of treatment accorded to those captured are not common in the chronicles, yet in several cases of Spaniards taken by the Indians there are no suggestions of torture.[23] An observation on the treatment of prisoners by the Guachoia [24] is interesting:

But they principally exercised their cruelty upon the suckling infants and upon old men; they first tore from the latter their clothes, and shot them to death with arrows which they generally aimed at the parts which show the difference of sex. As for the infants they threw them by the legs into the air, and shot them to death with their arrows before they fell to the ground.[25]

This is an excellent description of brutality without torture and suggests that had the torture practices noted more than 150 years later in the lower Mississippi region been present they would have been seen and commented upon by the Spaniards with De Soto.

The absence of reference to torture by the Indians does not complete the picture for the "Civilized" invaders unquestionably did practise it on the Indians for the customary European motives of abstracting information or supplies and as a punishment for refractory behavior. Some examples of this seem pertinent:

All the rest he commanded to be put to death, being tied to a stake in the midst of the market-place; and the Indians of Paracossi did shoot them to death.[26]

This treatment was a punishment for revolt. During the search for Cofitachequi:

. . . and he brought four or five Indians, and not one would show any knowledge of his lord's village or discover it, although they burnt one of them alive before the others, and all suffered that martyrdom for not revealing it.[27]

At Coste De Soto seized some chiefs:

[22] Swanton, *The Ethnological Value*, p. 576.
[23] Vega, p. 327.
[24] Identified by Swanton at Natchez, *Relation of the Southeast*, p. 63.
[25] Vega, p. 436.
[26] Elvas, p. 133. Also see Ranjel, p. 76.
[27] Ranjel, p. 97. Also see Elvas, p. 42.

. . . and he threatened them, and said that he would burn them all because they had laid hands on the Christians.[28]

While wintering the first year at Apalachee, Indians ambushed them often and:

. . . although the Spaniards pursued them and burned them they were never willing to make peace. If their hands and noses were cut off they made no more account of it. . . .[29]

Biedma mentions that they came to a large river which entered into the bay called Chuse and:

In the meanwhile the Indians killed one of the governor's guards. The governor punished the cacique for it, and threatened to burn him alive if he did not deliver up the murderers.[30]

While he was west of the Mississippi:

This Indian led him two days out of the way. The Governor commanded to torture him.[31]

At the time of boat building in the Natchez area the Governor feared a plot by some visiting Indians and consequently he ordered one to be detained secretly:

The Governor commanded him to be put to torture, to make him confess whether the Indians practise treason or no.[32]

Furthermore the Spaniards had fierce dogs used to track down and then tear the natives to pieces.[33] It is not difficult to believe that De Soto employed such methods on the Indians many times not recorded in the narratives. The stake and fire were common in Europe at that period. From the time of the earliest settlements in the West Indies Spanish brutality was a fact. Champlain on his trip to the West Indies and Mexico in 1599 not only speaks of Spaniards burning Indians but even furnishes a sketch showing it.[34]

Following De Soto there was a period of years during which many shipwrecks occurred on the southern end of Florida and the survivors were either slain or enslaved.[35] Among them was

[28] Ranjel, p. 110.
[29] Ranjel, p. 80.
[30] Biedma, p. 102. The threat against the cacique but not the mode of punishment is mentioned in Elvas, p. 199.
[31] He confessed and was cast to the dogs. Elvas, p. 199.
[32] Elvas, p. 204.
[33] Ranjel, p. 60, and Vega, p. 275, give descriptions of this.
[34] Champlain, I, p. 63 and Plate LX.
[35] Lowery, 1911, p. 352.

a boy, Fontaneda, who lived some seventeen years with the Indians until finally rescued in 1566. From him we have almost the only available account of the Calusa. No torture is mentioned and the following suggests its absence:

For the natives who took them (shipwrecked Spaniards) would order them to dance and sing; and as they were not understood and the Indians themselves are very artful—they thought the Christians were obstinate, and unwilling to do so. And so they would kill them, and report to the cacique that for their disobedience they had been slain.[36]

In 1559 a fleet of 13 vessels and 1500 people led by Tristan de Luna attempted to colonize northeastern Alabama after a preliminary exploration of the coast in 1558. They covered much of the Gulf Coast by land and water and finally fortified a settlement on Pensacola Bay.[37] Remains of towns destroyed by De Soto were seen and stragglers from his army found. An attempt was made in 1560 to penetrate into the interior in accordance with the original plans. They met with the Cocas [38] and aided them in a war against their enemy, the Napochies.[39] In a deserted Napochies village the Cocas:

. . . went from house to house looking for someone like infuriated lions and they found only a poor strange Indian . . . they tortured the poor Indian till they left him dying.[40]

This seems to have been rather a slaying than torture. Lowery uses the expression "despatched with blows" for the act.[41]

This colonization scheme failed, and when in 1561 Villafane offered to take those who wished to go with him to Saint Elena, the colony was deserted.[42] Villafane explored the coast of Georgia and Carolina for a short time but no contacts were made with the natives.[43]

French Hueguenots under the command of Ribault reached Florida [44] in 1562 and coasted northward to a large river named by them the River May and now identified as the St. Johns River.[45] Here they had friendly contact with the Indians and

[36] Fontaneda, p. 22.
[37] Lowery, 1911, pp. 358–359.
[38] The Coosa, a Creek tribe according to Swanton, *Early History*, p. 230.
[39] A Choctaw speaking tribe according to Swanton, *Southeastern Indians*, p. 5.
[40] Swanton, *Early History*, p. 237—citing Davila Padilla, *Historia*, pp. 205–217.
[41] Lowery, 1911, p. 367.
[42] Lowery, 1911, p. 374.
[43] Lowery, 1911, pp. 374–375.
[44] Near the present St. Augustine, Lowery, 1905, p. 32.
[45] Swanton, *Early History*, p. 48.

then proceeded north, finally establishing a small settlement at Port Royal near the present Beaufort, South Carolina,[46] which was soon abandoned. Little data on the Indians is found in the account of this voyage except that they were friendly and had greeted the French ". . . very gently and with great humanitie." [47]

A second French expedition under Laudonnière, who had accompanied Ribault previously, erected a fortified settlement on the St. Johns River in Florida in 1564. The artist Le Moyne accompanied this colony and his illustrations and descriptions together with the descriptions of Laudonnière furnish valuable material on the Timucua Indians. In spite of much information on war practices and ceremonials, torturing is not noted. On the contrary there is much to suggest its absence. A certain chief is spoken of as:

. . . a man cruell in warre, but pitiful in the execution of his furie. For hee tooke the prisoners to mercy, being content to mark them on the left arme with a great marke like unto a seale, . . . then hee let them goe without any more hurt.[48]

Immediate death for those taken in war was apparently customary [49] although some, particularly women and children, might be taken prisoners.[50] Charlevoix sums up the Florida Indians, not however from personal experience, as follows:

They are not as cruel to their prisoners as those of Canada; and although, like the latter, cannibals, they do not carry inhumanity so far as to make the sufferings of a miserable wretch a spectacle of pleasure, or torture an art. Women and children taken in war, they are satisfied with keeping in slavery; men they immolate to the sun, and deem it a religious duty to eat the flesh of these victims.[51]

Ribault arrived in Florida on a second voyage in 1565 bringing much needed aid to the year-old colony but was not able to prevent its destruction by the Spanish under Mendenez. In 1567 Gourges led a French expedition to avenge the massacre and succeeded in destroying a Spanish settlement in the vicinity of the present St. Augustine. Both of these expeditions used

[46] Lowery, 1905, p. 402—Swanton, *Early History*, p. 49.
[47] Ribault, p. 101.
[48] Laudonnière, p. 458.
[49] Le Moyne, p. 7—Laudonnière, pp. 413, 494.
[50] Laudonnière, pp. 464, 469.
[51] Charlevoix, *History and General Description*, I, p. 138.

ɪndian allies in their ruthless warfare but there are no accusations of Indian cruelty.[52]

Mendenez made extended explorations along the coast of Florida and the Pardo expedition penetrated far into the interior of Georgia. Forts and Missions were established by force of arms. Little ethnography is found in the records and there are no accounts of Indian cruelty.[53] The Missions established by Mendenez among the Calusa and Timucua of Florida, and among the Guale of the coast of Georgia, suffered many privations and sustained much conflict with the Indians in which numerous whites were slain. Any idea of retaliation by torture on the part of the Indians was apparently lacking. The Jesuit Missionaries left on Chesapeake Bay in 1570 initially had peaceful relations with the natives but were later slaughtered, as far as can be ascertained, without torture. When Mendenez attempted to succor this Virginia Mission in 1571 he caught eight Indians whom he hung for the murder of the Jesuits.[54]

Upon the return of the first voyage sent to America under the command of Captain Barlowe, at the instigation of Sir Walter Raleigh in 1584, the Indians in the vicinity of Pamlico Sound, North Carolina, were reported as kind and loving.[55] While little weight can be attached to a statement which was propaganda for colonization, nevertheless there is no indication in any of the accounts of the later voyages in 1585, 1586 and 1587 under Lane and White or in the descriptions of Hariot, all of which contain excellent ethnographic material, of torture being practised by the Indians.

The Indians of Guale, Georgia, rose in rebellion against the Spanish Missions in 1597 and killed many priests and Christianized Indians, apparently without torture except in the case of a Father who had been kept as a slave and then:

"They tied him to a post and put much wood under him." [56] He was spared finally and exchanged for a prisoner held by the Spaniards.[57]

[52] For an account of this French-Spanish conflict see Laudonnière, *A Notable Historie,* and Lowery, 1905.

[53] See Lowery, 1905, for an account of these explorations.

[54] For a discussion of these Missions see Lowery, 1905, pp. 339 f.

[55] Barlowe, *The First Voyage.*

[56] Swanton, *Early History,* p. 87—citing Barcia.

[57] For an account of this rebellion see Swanton, *Early History,* pp. 85 f.—citing Barcia.

The accounts of Spelman, Percy, Strachey, Smith, and later Beverley, of the English settlements in Virginia give no indication that any of the Southeastern Algonkians used torture on captives. Fear on the part of the whites of suffering such a fate seems to have been entirely absent. There is however a suggestion that these Indians were familiar with the Iroquois torturing:

For the heads of all those rivers, especially the Pattawomekes, the Pauturuntes, the Sasquesahanocks, the Tockwoughes, are continually tormeted by them (the Massawomekes, or Five Nation Iroquois) : of whose crueltie, they generally complained. . . .[58]

Percy likewise reports that Powhatan:

. . . described also upon the same Sea (to the west), a mighty Nation called Pocoughtronack, a fierce Nation that did eate men, and warred with the people. . . .[59]

Men were evidently seldom taken captive by Southeastern Algonkians but Smith remarks:

Yet the Werowances, women and children, they put not to death, but keepe them captives.[60]

Slaughter of all enemies seems to have been the more general rule:

. . . they destroy man, woman, and child, to prevent all future resentments.[61]

Smith, and later Beverley, emphasized that neither age nor sex was spared in the massacre of the English instigated by Oppechancanough in 1622 but that all were immediately slain.[62] Smith further elaborates upon this tragedy of 1622:

. . . they fell againe upon the dead bodies, making as well as they could a fresh murder, defacing, dragging, and mangling their carkases into many peeces, and carrying some parts away in derision, ...[63]

The resentment on the part of the Indians indicated by such behavior would surely have resulted in torturing if the practice had been known to them.

[58] Smith, *A Map of Virginia,* p. 105.
[59] Percy, p. 49.
[60] Smith, *A Map of Virginia,* p. 106.   Also mentioned by Strachey, p. 107.
[61] Beverley, p. 150.
[62] Smith, *The Generall Historie,* p. 358.   Beverley, p. 40.
[63] Smith, *The Generall Historie,* p. 359.

Smith himself cites a case where he applied torture to an Indian:

The Counsell concluded, that I should terrifie them with some torture, to know if I could know their intent. The next day, I bound one in hold to the maine Mast: and presenting sixe Muskets . . . forced him to desire life. . . . I affrighted the other, first with the rack, then with Muskets; . . . .[64]

A letter dated 1611 from the Rev. Alexander Whitaker, who was in Virginia, attempts to dissuade Dale from exploration by citing the dangers:

. . . otherwise he (Powhatan) threatened to destroy us after a strange manner. First hee said hee would make us dumbe and then kill us. . . .[65]

Had torture been practised it would have made a much more efficacious deterrent.

Exploration of Carolina by Bland in 1650 seems to have been without any fear of torture from the Nottaway, Meherrin and Tuscarora, all of whom were Iroquois speaking. Lederer in his travels during 1669 and 1670 does not seem to have observed torturing. By 1674 English traders were penetrating far inland and one of them, Gabriel Arther, was captured by the Tomahitans, who were probably Yuchi, and:

. . . tied . . . to a stake and laid heaps of combustible canes about him to burn him. . . .[66]

In a letter dated 1675 a Bishop of Cuba describes the Indians of Florida but gives only one incident, and that from hearsay, which might be construed as torture. This referred to a tribe along the northern borders of Florida, the Chichimecos, identified by Swanton as probably Yuchi.[67]

. . . so savage and cruel that their only concern is to assault villages, Christian and Heathen, taking lives and sparing neither age, sex nor estate, roasting and eating victims.[68]

As this is at best a second-hand account of a non-Christian tribe by a Spanish Bishop, too much weight cannot be attached to it. Furthermore, straight cannibalism rather than torture may be indicated.

[64] Smith, *A True Relation*, p. 67.
[65] Bushnell, *Virginia from Early Records*, p. 36.
[66] Alvord, p. 218.
[67] Wenhold, p. 4.
[68] Wenhold, p. 11.

An account of a war between the Apalachee and the Yuchi contained in a letter dated 1678 does not suggest the use of torture on the vanquished Yuchi by the Apalachee.[69]

It is only with the account by Lawson of his journey in Carolina in 1700 that we get any definite torture referred to in this section. He states that few prisoners of the Saponi, who were Eastern Siouans, escaped having lighted splinters stuck in their bodies, and then being made to dance around a fire until dead.[70]   Failure to so treat prisoners in one case resulted in a terrific storm sent by the "devil." [71]   Speaking in general of the Indians of North Carolina Lawson says they invented horrible cruelties prolonged as long as possible. Ignited pine splinters stuck in the body of the victim, dancing, derision, buffeting until death, and final dismemberment were usual.[72]   A Huguenot traveler met the Saponi in 1715 and accuses them of inhumanly murdering all their prisoners, but does not specifically describe torture.[73]   Criminals were cruelly executed by a special official in front of the rejoicing population.[74]

Lawson was himself killed by the Tuscarora in 1711. His companion Graffenreid, who was spared, does not report the method used other than to say that he was condemned to have his throat cut with his own razor.[75]

In 1704 the English waged a war of extermination against the Indians during which the Apalachee tied some other Indians to stakes and burned them alive.[76]

The earliest descriptions of Creek torturing are contained in Dr. Hewit's accounts of the cruelties practised upon captives by the Yamassee who were then raiding the Spanish settlements in Florida from their home on the north side of the Savannah River just prior to the war of 1715:

The Yamassees possessed a large territory lying backward from Port-Royal island, on the north-east side of Savanna river, ... For many years they had been accustomed to make incursions into the Spanish territories, and to wage war with the Indians within their bounds. In their return from those southern expeditions, it had been a common practice

[69] Swanton, *Early History*, pp. 299 f.
[70] Lawson, p. 47.
[71] Lawson, p. 49.
[72] Lawson, pp. 197 f.
[73] Fontaine, p. 279.
[74] Lawson, pp. 195 f.
[75] Williamson, I, pp. 285–286.
[76] Swanton, *Early History*, p. 123—citing a letter from a Spanish Governor.

with them to lurk in the woods round Augustine, until they surprised some Spaniard, and brought him prisoner to their towns. On the bodies of these unfortunate prisoners they were accustomed to exercise the most wanton barbarities; sometimes cutting them to pieces slowly, joint by joint, with knives and tomahawks; at other times burying them up to the neck underground, then standing at a distance and marking at their heads with their pointed arrows; and, at other times, binding them to a tree, and piercing the tenderest parts of their naked bodies with sharp-pointed sticks of burning wood, which last, because the most painful and excruciating method of torture, was the most common among them.[77]

However, the Yamassee and their allies united with the Spanish to drive out the English in 1715. The English captives were sometimes tortured:

John Cochran, his wife, and four children; Mr. Bray, his wife, and two children; and six more men and women, having found some friends among them, were spared for some days; but, while attempting to make their escape from them, they were retaken and put to death. Such as had no friends among them were tortured in the most shocking manner, the Indians seeming to neglect their progress towards conquest on purpose to assist in tormenting their enemies. We forbear to mention the various tortures inflicted on such as fell into their merciless fangs.[78]

After the English had driven the Yamassee south into Florida they still continued raiding into Carolina:

One party of them catched William Hooper, and killed him by degrees, by cutting off one joint of his body after another until he expired. Another party surprised Henry Quinton, Thomas Simmons, and Thomas Parmenter, and, to gratify their revenge, tortured them to death.[79]

No other cases of torture are found in the documents collected by Carroll, and none of the ones cited above were reported by eye-witnesses. The Creek and Cherokee wars, which were extremely bitter against the whites, did not bring out any incidents of torturing.

The French explorers and missionaries gradually pushed westward from the St. Lawrence during the 17th century and journeyed down the Mississippi River. Marquette and Joliet in 1673 made many ethnological observations, especially on the Illinois, but without noting any torture practices.

Tonty's accounts of La Salle's journey down the Mississippi starting in 1678, and of the search until 1691 for La Salle after

[77] Carroll, I, pp. 189–191.
[78] Carroll, I, p. 197.
[79] Carroll, I, p. 199.

his fatal attempt to find the mouth of the river, lack any reference to torture by the tribes along the lower reaches of the Mississippi or among the Caddo to the west. Illinois [80] and Iroquois [81] were, on the contrary, both accused of the practice. Hennepin, who accompanied La Salle part of the time, likewise reported torturing by the Iroquois,[82] but also does not refer to it further south. La Salle's attempt to locate the mouth of the Mississippi from the Gulf of Mexico is described in the accounts of Joutel from which most of the early ethnography of the Caddo of eastern Texas and Louisiana is derived. The Hasinai apparently slew most of their enemies immediately. There is, however, an incident of a woman captive who:

. . . was kept to fall a sacrifice to the rage and vengeance of the women and maids; who, having armed themselves with thick sticks, sharp pointed at the end, conducted that wretch to a by-place, where each of those furies began to torment her, sometimes with the point of their staff, and sometimes laying on her with all their might. One tore off her hair, another cut off her finger, and every one of those outrageous women endeavored to put her to some exquisite torture, to avenge the death of their husbands and kinsmen, who had been killed in the former wars; so that the unfortunate creature expected her death stroke as mercy.

At last, one of them gave her a stroke with a heavy club on the head, and another ran her stake several times into her body, with which she fell down dead on the spot. Then they cut that miserable victim into morsels, and obliged some slaves of that nation they had been long possessed of, to eat them.[83]

This is the only account in Joutel which could be interpreted as indicative of torture.

Excellent descriptions of the Southern Caddoans are furnished in the letters of early Spanish Missionaries to eastern Texas in 1691, 1716, and 1722, but only one slight reference to torture is mentioned by these men who lived in intimacy with and constant danger from the Indians. In 1691 Fray Franciso Casanas de Jesus Maria wrote of the Tejas (Hasinai) as follows:

In conclusion it may be said that these Indians practice no greater cruelty than their enemies do. They tie a captive's feet and hands to a post like a cross. Here they tear him to pieces, drinking the blood and eating the flesh half roasted.[84]

[80] Tonty, *Memoir*, p. 65.
[81] Tonty, *Memoir*, p. 56.
[82] Hennepin, p. 198.
[83] Joutel, *Historical Journal*, p. 160. See also *Relation*, pp. 379–380.
[84] Hatcher, 30, p. 217.

This has interesting connotations and will be discussed more fully elsewhere. It confirms Joutel's observations on cannibalism in this region but it is questionable whether it should be identified as torture. Hidalgo and Espinosa do not mention it.[85]

An interesting account is furnished by Morfi for the Taovayas, a Southern Caddoan tribe:

. . . are excessively cruel with captives; . . . and this cruelty on their part is more an impudent reprisal, . . . than a ferocious spirit, because they only exercise it with those nations who treat their prisoners with the same barbarity; and up to the present it is not known. On the contrary, they feast them and hold them to esteem in proportion to the valor they show in their defense, ...[86]

When Gravier voyaged down the Mississippi about 1700 he commented upon the torture practices of the Iroquois,[87] but on none lower down the river. He specifically exempts the Houma from such cruelty.[88]

The accounts of d'Iberville of the first French Settlements on the Gulf beginning in 1699, which were under his command, give little ethnographic data and no indication of torture. The missionary Ru who accompanied him is much more informative, but has no remarks on any kind of torture, although several cases of human sacrifice, which will be discussed later, were noted by him. He does not suggest that any cruelty was associated with the deaths of fifty Colapissa warriors at the hands of the Chickasaw.[89]

Penicaut visited this region about 1704. He gives a description of cannibalism by the Hasinai during which the victim was secured to a frame. Torture, aside from the eating of the victim while still alive, apparently did not accompany it.[90] He also mentions that seventeen Spaniards were taken as prisoners to Mobile in 1719 and clubbed to death, which is perhaps evidence that torture was not used by this group.[91] However, Penicaut furnishes the earliest description of torture known for this region:

[85] See Hatcher.
[86] Morfi, p. 11.
[87] *Jesuit Relations*, **65**, pp. 35–37.
[88] *Jesuit Relations*, **65**, p. 151.
[89] Ru, p. 66.
[90] Penicaut, *Annals*, p. 121.
[91] Penicaut, *Annals*, p. 148.

These savages who are named Coroas, are the most cruel of all those of
Louisiana.   They are almost always hunting or at war, and when they
have taken one of their enemies alive, they fasten him to a frame, which
is composed of two poles 8 feet in height, 5 feet apart, the two hands
being well bound above and the two feet below, in the form of a St.
Andrew's cross.   The poor wretch being fastened thus completely naked,
the entire village collects around him.   They have a fire lighted in this
place, where they have placed pieces of iron such as old gun barrels,
shovels, or the iron part of axes and other similar things, to make them
red hot, and when they are thoroughly reddened they rub them upon his
back, arms, thighs, and legs; they then lay bare the skin all around his
head as far as the ears, tearing it off from him by force.   They fill this
skin with burning coals, which they replace on his head; they put the ends
of his fingers into their lighted pipes, which they smoke, and tear out his
nails, tormenting him thus until he is dead.[92]

The Coroas, or Koroa, were a group speaking the Tunican
language.   The fact that their cruelty impressed Penicaut as
unusual suggests the rarity if not the absence of torture in the
region.   The related Tunica were accused of burning a Natchez
woman on a frame set up in New Orleans with the permission
of the French.[93]

La Harpe, who settled in Louisiana in 1718, is a reasonably
full source for the Caddo and other Texas tribes.   He gives
nothing on torture for this region, although he does repeat a
report that the Quapaw had burned some Iroquois alive in 1706.[94]

Charlevoix, visiting the lower Mississippi in 1721–1722,
states that it was the fate of all Natchez captives to be burned.
He supplies no details other than that these captives were first
compelled to dance in front of the temple.[95]   The Quapaw are
accused by him also of burning those prisoners not saved for
adoption.[96]

Le Petit repeats the same brief description of Natchez torture as recorded by Charlevoix.[97]   It is only with the very full
account by Du Pratz that we get a satisfactory picture of the
actual treatment of a victim:

If they are able to carry away any of the enemies of their nation they
are received honorably.   If these are women or children they are en-

92 Penicaut, *Relation*, pp. 458–459.
93 Romans, p. 96.
94 Harpe, p. 35.
95 Charlevoix, *Historical Journal*, p. 167.
96 Charlevoix, *Historical Journal*, p. 128.
97 *Jesuit Relations*, **68**, p. 149.

slaved. They serve in this capacity after their hair has been cut extremely short. But if it is a man that they have made prisoner the joy is general and their glory is at its height. On arriving near their nation they make the war cry three times repeated, and in this case, however wearied the warriors may be, they go at once to hunt for the three poles which are necessary for the construction of the fatal instrument on which they are going to make the enemy they have taken die, I mean the frame (cadre) on which they cruelly immolate the unfortunate victim of their vengeance.

Of these three poles which are about ten feet long, two are set in the earth. They are straight and a good pace apart from each other. They assure themselves that they are firmly placed. The third is cut in halves in order to cross the two that are already planted. The first is 2 feet above the earth and the other 5 feet above the first. These poles, thus adjusted and bound together as strongly as possible as is necessary, form, indeed, a frame, and it is from that fact that the French have taken a name of this gallows machine. The natives tie the victim to the foot of this frame,[98] and when he is there he sings the death song until his scalp is taken. After the warriors have thus tied him they are permitted to go to eat. The victim, if he so desires, may then take his last meal. The old warriors guard him. Each one can look at him, but he is not allowed to speak to him, still less to insult him.

When the warriors have finished their meal they come to the place where the frame is planted to which the victim is tied. They make him advance a little and turn his entire body around in order that the people may see him. The one who has taken him gives a blow of his wooden war club below the back part of his head, making the death cry while removing the scalp in the best manner he is able without tearing it.

After the scalp has been taken from the victim, they tie a cord to each of his wrists, throw the ends of the cords over the crosspiece, which many take and draw in order to pull him up while others lift him, placing his feet on the crosspiece below and tying him to the corners of the square. They do the same to his hands at the upper corners of the square in such a manner that the victim in this position has his body free and entirely bare, and the four limbs form a St. Andrew's cross.

From the time they begin to take the scalp from the victim the young people go in search of dry canes, crush them, and make packages or bundles of the entire length of the canes which they bind in many places. They bring other dry canes, also, which have been neither crushed nor bound which the warriors make use of against the victim.

The one who took him is the first one to take a single crushed cane, light it and burn the place he may choose. But he devotes himself especially to burn the arm with which he (the prisoner) had best defended himself. Another comes and burns another place. These, with their pipes filled with dry and burning tobacco, burn him about the foot. Those heat a nail red hot, with which they pierce his foot. All, in fact,

[98] For an illustration of this ''cadre'' see Du Pratz, II, p. 429. Dumont, p. 78, states that the frame was located in front of the temple.

one after the other, revenge themselves as best they are able on this victim, who, so long as strength remains to him, employs it in singing the death song, which, when closely examined, is found to consist of grievous cries, tears, and groans. Usage decides and governs everything.

Some have been seen to sing and suffer continually during three days and three nights without anyone giving them a glass of water to quench their thirst, and it is not permitted to anyone to give it to them, even should they ask for it, which they never do, without doubt, because they know that the hearts of their enemies are inflexible. In fact, it must be admitted that if the natives are good friends during peace, they are in war irreconcilable enemies.

It sometimes happens that a young woman who may have lost her husband in war, seeing the victim when he arrives completely naked and without means of concealing his defects, if he has any, demands him for her husband, and he is granted to her on the spot.

It also happens that when he suffers too long a pitying woman lights a cane torch, and when it is burning well, makes him die in an instant by putting this torch to the most sensitive place, and the tragic scene is in this way ended.[99]

In his account of the 1729 massacre of the French by the Natchez, Dumont does not indicate that any were tortured, but a few days later a white was burned on the frame, evidently subjected to the treatment described by Du Pratz.[100] In 1730 a French woman was burned.[101]

Bossu does not refer to the Natchez as torturing, but he gives an account of Illinois cruelty to both Fox Indians and Englishmen.[102] He likewise accuses the Quapaw of torturing.[103]

The French seem not only to have countenanced cruelty on the part of their Indian allies, but even to have indulged in such behavior themselves, for in a letter of Governor Perier after the Natchez rebellion there is the following remark:

Latterly I burned four men, and two women, and sent the rest to St. Domingo.[104]

There are conflicting reports about the Choctaw during the eighteenth century. Le Petit reports that they burned some Negroes alive in 1730,[105] and an early anonymous account of

[99] Du Pratz, II, pp. 428–432.
[100] Dumont, pp. 78 f.
[101] Dumont, p. 98.
[102] Bossu, I, pp. 130, 186.
[103] Bossu, I, pp. 105 f.
[104] Gayarre, I, p. 438.
[105] *Jesuit Relations*, **68**, p. 199.

Louisiana, translated by Swanton, dating from the early part of the century states:

When they are able to bring home prisoners, they have them burned at their village, and it is a great joy to them when this happens.[106]

On the contrary, Romans clears the Choctaw of any such cruelty:

They never exercised so much cruelty as the other savages; they almost always brought them home to show them, and then dispatched them with a bullet or hatchet.[107]

He contrasts this conduct with that of the Creeks whom he accuses of permitting hardly a captive to escape terrible tortures.[108] Dumont gives an incident of the Choctaw burning a Natchez woman whom they tied to a bundle of canes when they were aiding the French to avenge the massacre of 1729.[109]

In 1756 a Colapissa was surrendered to the Choctaw to replace a murdered man. This man was killed in great anger but without torture.[110]

In 1722 four Frenchmen and an Indian slave were captured by the Chickasaw. They wrote that their captors were treating them well:

This is surely a sign that the Indians want peace, for when a prisoner cannot work, it is their custom to kill them.[111]

The earliest account of Chickasaw torture refers to the time of the French war against them in 1736 when twenty-six French soldiers and seven officers were tied to stakes and burned by slow fires.[112]

By far the most complete account of Chickasaw torture, and, in fact, for any Mushkogean tribe, is given by Adair who traded in this region after 1736 and upon whom we must rely for much of our data on Southeastern warfare. The following is his description of the Chickasaw torture of a prisoner:

It has been long too feelingly known, that instead of observing the generous and hospitable part of the laws of war, and saving the unfortunate

---

106 Swanton, *An Early Account*, p. 67.
107 Romans, p. 75.
108 Romans, p. 97.
109 Dumont, p. 89.
110 Bossu, I, p. 171.
111 Mereness, pp. 31, 33.
112 Bossu, I, p. 311—Dumont, p. 114.

who fall into their power, that they generally devote their captives to death, with the most agonizing tortures. No representation can possibly be given, so shocking to humanity, as their unmerciful method of tormenting their devoted prisoner; and as it so contrary to the standard of the rest of the known world, I shall relate the circumstances, so far as to convey proper information thereof to the reader. When the company return from war, and come in view of their own town, they follow the leader one by one, in a direct line, each a few yards behind the other, to magnify their triumph. If they have not succeeded, or any of their warriors are lost, they return quite silent; but if they are all safe, and have succeeded, they fire off the Indian platoon, by one, two, and three at a time, whooping and insulting their prisoners. They camp near their town all night, in a large square plot of ground, marked for the purpose, with a high war-pole fixed in the middle of it, to which they secure their prisoners. Next day they go to the leader's house in a very solemn procession, but they stay without, round his red-painted war-pole, till they have determined concerning the fate of their prisoners. If any one of the captives should be fortunate enough to get loose, run into the house of the arch-magus, or to a town of refuge, he by ancient custom, is saved from the fiery torture—these places being a sure asylum to them if they were invaded, and taken, but not to invaders, because they came to shed blood.

The young prisoners are saved, if not devoted while the company was sanctifying themselves for their expedition; but if the latter be the case, they are condemned, and tied to the dreadful stake, one at a time. The victors first strip their miserable captives, and put on their feet a pair of bear-skin maccaseenes, with the black hairy part outwards; others fasten with a grape-vine, a burning fire-brand to the pole, a little above the reach of their heads. Then they know their doom—deep black, and burning fire, are fixed seals of their death-warrant. Their punishment is always left to the women; and on account of their false standard of education, they are no way backward in their office, but perform it to the entire satisfaction of the greedy eyes of the spectators. Each of them prepares for the dreadful rejoicing, a long bundle of dry canes, or the heart of fat pitch-pine, and as the victims are lead to the stake, the women and their young ones beat them with these in a most barbarous manner. Happy would it be for the miserable creatures, if their sufferings ended here, or a merciful tomahawk finished them at one stroke; but this shameful treatment is a prelude to future sufferings.

The death signal being given, preparations are made for acting a more tragic part. The victim's arms are fast pinioned, and a strong grape-vine is tied around his neck, to the top of the war-pole, allowing him to track around, about fifteen yards. They fix some tough clay on his head, to secure the scalp from the blazing torches. Unspeakable pleasure now fills the exulting crowd of spectators, and the circle fills with the Amazon and merciless executioners. The suffering warrior however is not dismayed; with an exulting manly voice he sings the war song! And with gallant contempt he tramples the rattling gourd with pebbles in it to pieces, and outbraves even death itself. The women make a furious onset with their burning torches; his pain is soon so excruciating, that he rushes out from the pole, with the fury of the most savage beast of prey, and with the vine sweeps down all before him, kicking, biting, and trampling them, with the greatest despite. The circle immediately fills again, either with the same, or fresh persons; they attack him on every side—now he runs to the pole for shelter, but the flames pursue him. Then with champing teeth, and sparkling eye-balls, he breaks through their contracted circle afresh, and acts every part, that the highest courage, most raging fury, and blackest despair can prompt him to. But he is sure to be overpowered by numbers, and after some time the fire affects his tender parts. Then they pour over him a quantity of cold water, and allow him a proper time of respite, till his spirits recover, and he is capable of suffering new tortures. Then the like cruelties are repeated till he falls down, and happily becomes insensible of pain. Now they scalp him, in the manner before described; dismember, and carry off all the exterior branches of the body (pudendis non exceptis), in shameful, and savage triumph. This is the most favorable treatment their devoted captives receive; it would be too shocking to humanity either to give, or peruse, every particular of their conduct in such doleful tragedies—nothing can equal these scenes, but those of the merciful Romanish inquisition.

Not a soul, of whatever age or sex, manifests the least pity during the prisoner's tortures; the women sing with religious joy, all the while they are torturing the devoted victim, and peals of laughter resound through the crowded theatre—especially if he fears to die. But a warrior puts on a bold austere countenance, and carries it through all his pains;—as long as he can, he whoops and outbraves the enemy, describing his own martial deeds against them, and those of his nation, who he threatens will force many of them to eat fire in revenge of his fate, as he himself had often done to some of their relations at their cost.[113]

Except for the above, Adair gives few details of actual torturing, merely mentioning that all Indians practised such cruelties.[114] All captives were not tortured, for Adair indicates that only those who were pretty well advanced in life were so treated.[115] However, the enemy might be "devoted" to death prior to the setting out of the war party. The warriors made a vow to kill all met on a certain trail, or during a certain time, or belonging to a certain nation.[116] This devotion to death did not specifically require torture but perhaps might sometimes include it. A prisoner, whether or not condemned to torture, could be saved by escaping to a town of refuge or to the house

[113] Adair, pp. 388–391.
[114] Adair, p. 154.
[115] Adair, p. 389.
[116] Adair, p. 155.

of the Arch-magus.[117] These towns of refuge, or White Towns, offered a haven to criminals as well as to captives [118] in contrast to the Red, or War, Towns which Swanton has suggested were a recent addition by migration to the culture.[119]

Adair furnishes the following account of the Cherokee torturing a party of Mohawks who had raided southward in 1747, his information coming from a trader supposedly among the Choctaw at the time:

But they were overpowered by numbers, captivated, and put to the most exquisite tortures of fire, amidst a prodigious crowd of exulting foes. . . . when they were tied to the stake, the younger of the two discovering our traders on a hill pretty near, addressed them in English, and entreated them to redeem their lives. The elder immediately spoke to him, in his own language, to desist—on this he collected himself, and became composed like a stoic, manifesting an indifference to life or death, pleasure or pain, according to their standard of martial virtue: and their dying behavior did not reflect the least dishonor on their former gallant actions. All the pangs of fiery torture served only to refine their manly spirits; and as it was out of the power of the traders to redeem them, they according to our usual custom retired, as soon as the Indians began the diabolical tragedy.[120]

A traditional account of Cherokee torture of a Seneca chief furnishes perhaps the most detail:

They (the Cherokee) tied him (the Seneca chief) and carried him to two women of the tribe who had the power to decide what should be done with him. . . . They decided to burn the soles of his feet until they were blistered, then to put grains of corn under the skin and to chase him with clubs until they had beaten him to death.

They stripped him and burnt his feet. Then they tied a bark rope around his waist, with an old man to hold the other end, and made him run between two lines of people, with clubs in their hands. When they gave the word to start . . . (he escaped).[121]

The above account is interesting mainly for the reference to the power of deciding the fate of captives invested in the ''Be-

[117] Adair, pp. 156, 161, 417.
[118] Schoolcraft, V, p. 279—Bartram, *Travels*, p. 389.
[119] Swanton, *Social Organization*, pp. 274 f.
[120] Adair, p. 384.
[121] Mooney, *Myths*, p. 360. Dr. Fenton has kindly communicated to the writer a practically identical tradition obtained by him in 1934 from John Jimmerson, except that it applied to the Choctaw, not the Cherokee. About the time of the wars of 1750–1760 a Seneca chief was captured, had both his feet blistered, and then escaped from the row of warriors. The principal difference between these traditions, other than the identity of the enemy, is in the condemnation to torture. In the case of the Choctaw this was done by a council of warriors.

loved Women'' and is confirmed by Timberlake who was with the Cherokee about 1760:

Old warriors likewise, or war-women, who can no longer go to war, but have distinguished themselves in their younger days, have the title of Beloved. This is the only titles females can enjoy; but it abundantly recompenses them, by the power they acquire by it which is so great that they can, by the wave of a swan's wing, deliver a wretch condemned by the council and already tied to the stake.[122]

In 1776 they threatened to torture a white woman:

She was bound, taken to the top of one of the mounds, and was about to be burned, when Nancy Ward, then exercising in the nation the functions of the Beloved or Pretty Woman, interfered and pronounced her pardon.[123]

During this same campaign instigated by the British the Cherokees captured a boy:

Moore (the boy) was carried prisoner to the Indian towns, and was tortured to death by burning.[124]

The ferocious reputation of the Cherokee among the Whites of Carolina is perhaps best expressed by Logan:

. . . the midnight alarms and horrid butcheries of helpless women and children, and the terrible scenes of their more dreadful tortures in captivity and at the stake, have not yet received due notice at the hands of any chronicler.[125]

Nevertheless, there is no adequate description of the torture practices available. It cannot be too explicitly assumed that a stake was actually used because Indian torture was often characterized as burning at the stake although in most cases there was no actual binding of the captive.

Adair also refers to an English narrative stating that the Shawnee tortured men, women and children, but did not attempt the chastity of women for fear of offending their god.[126] Shawnee torture of a Creek is mentioned without details.[127] A rather full description of the torture of an Iroquois appears in Adair:

[122] Timberlake, p. 71.
[123] Ramsey, p. 157.
[124] Ramsey, p. 158.
[125] Logan, p. 205.
[126] Adair, p. 164.
[127] Adair, p. 392—Logan, pp. 250–251.

The Shawano also captivated a warrior of the Anantooeah, and put him
to the stake, according to their usual cruel solemnities.   Having uncon-
cernedly suffered much sharp torture, he told them with scorn, they did
not know how to punish a noted enemy, therefore he was willing to teach
them, and would confirm the truth of his assertion, if they allowed him
the opportunity.   Accordingly he requested of them a pipe and some
tobacco, which was given him : as soon as he lighted it, he sat down, naked
as he was, on the women's burning torches, that were within his circle,
and continued smoking his pipe without the least discomposure—on this
a head warrior leaped up, and said they had seen plain enough, that he
was a warrior, and not afraid of dying ; nor should he have died, only
that he was both spoiled by the fire, and devoted to it by their laws :
however, though he was a very dangerous enemy, and his nation a
treacherous people, it should appear that they paid a regard to bravery,
even in one who was marked over the body with war streaks, at the cost
of many lives of their beloved kindred.   And then by way of favor, he,
with his friendly tomahawk, instantly put an end to all his pains :—
though the merciful but bloody instrument was ready some minutes
before he gave the blow, yet I was assured, the spectators could not
perceive the sufferer to change, either his posture, or his steady erect
countenance, in the least.[128]

Shortly after Mary Jemison's capture by the Shawnee in
1755, she saw the fragments of burnt bodies hanging on a pole
in a Shawnee village on the banks of the Ohio.[129]   She describes
how the Shawnee tortured a white captive in 1759 for what she
believed to be the sole purpose of exulting at his distress :

They first made him stand up, while they slowly pared his ears, and split
them into strings.   They then made a number of slight incisions in his
face, and bound him on the ground, rolled him in the dirt, and rubbed
it in his wounds, some of them at the same time whipping him with small
rods.[130]

Mary Jemison, at this time an adopted Iroquois, persuaded
them to release him.

In 1782 the Shawnee burned the British Officer Crawford.
A council decided his fate which was to be fastened by the wrists
to a thick post in the midst of a circle of fire and slowly roasted.
Squaws also threw embers on him.   This proceeding was watched
with pleasure by the renegade Simon Girty.[131]   A captive was
tied to a tree in 1790 and embers applied to deep cuts made in

---

[128] Adair, pp. 392–393.
[129] Seaver, p. 56.
[130] Seaver, p. 75.
[131] Seaver, pp. 194 f.

his body. He was then released and killed by torches applied to his bowels.[132]

Ridout describes the torturing by the Shawnee of a captive who had been given to one of the warriors in 1788. This warrior wished to kill him instead of adopting him. The victim ran out of a house, entirely naked and with his ears cut off. The Indians chased him to a hill where he was tortured by fire for three hours until dead. Later the wigwams were "beaten" to drive away the spirits of the dead.[133]

In 1790 Hay was surprised that a captive taken to avenge the murder of a Shawnee had been adopted rather than burned, a fate which he believed was inflicted in all such cases.[134]

The Prophet told Trowbridge that he had witnessed the burning of two white men about 1794 near Fort Wayne. No fire was kindled to hasten their deaths but they were slowly killed with brands. All prisoners painted black before their arrival in the village were tortured unless released by the great peace woman.[134a] A tradition states that a Cannibalistic Society burned and ate prisoners although it is not clear that the burning took place while the victim was alive.[134b]

A pseudo-historical account of Shawnee torture was obtained in 1935 by Dr. E. Voegelin from her informant. The bravery of the Catawba victims is emphasized, and the method of burning them is unique in this region. They were compelled to walk back and forth in a small space surrounded by fire. It was also stated that one division of the Shawnee were not allowed to burn captives.[135]

When Milfort arrived among the Creeks in the latter part of the eighteenth century he said he found them still practising torture by burning their captives and that he persuaded them to abandon the custom.[136] Bartram describes the Chunky Yards of the Creeks with their "slave posts" to which captives condemned to be burned had once been tied but which were stated to be no longer in use although some old traders remembered such burnings.[137] He saw no such Chunky Yards in the Chero-

132 Spencer, p. 16.
133 Edgar, pp. 363–364.
134 Hay, p. 248.
134a Voegelin, p. 21.
134b Voegelin, pp. 53 f., 64.
135 Personal communication through the kindness of Dr. E. Voegelin.
136 Milfort, p. 219.
137 Bartram, *Observations*, pp. 35–36.

kee towns but found remains of them in the ancient sites.[138]   In another place, Bartram was assured by the oldest traders that they had never seen an instance of burning though they said it had occurred formerly.[139]   He was told by an old Spaniard that both the Creeks and the Spaniards had been cruel to prisoners, and that the Indians had burned captives to appease the spirits of their slain relatives.[140]

Swan does not describe Creek torture but its occurrence may be inferred from his statement that captives who succeeded in reaching a town of refuge escaped such a fate.[141]   In Hawkin's accounts of the Creeks in the period between 1796 and 1806 no references are made to torture.   Recent informants of Swanton said they still remembered the Creek slave posts for securing torture victims,[142] and also told him a tradition that the Indians of Alabama had once tortured one of their own tribe who had been adopted by the Choctaw and had then fought against his own people.[143]

Speck was told by informants in 1906 that the Yuchi had burned captives at the stake in the square grounds, the captor having the right to determine the fate of his prisoner.[144]

Archæological evidences of torture or human sacrifice from the mounds is very inconclusive.   Thomas thought that there were some indications of the practice in Illinois and Tennessee, based upon occasional remains of burnt stakes and associated charred bones.[145]   He did not believe that this indicated human sacrifice,[146] but the basis for such a fine distinction is not evident. More recently Shetrone concluded:

Despite the fact that early writers attributed human sacrifice to the Hopewell and other highly evolved mound-building peoples, there is no real evidence and scant probability that it was practised among them.[147]

Contact of Indian and White in the north was much more

---

[138] Bartram, *Observations,* p. 36—Swanton was told by informants that these posts were still faintly remembered as being in the shape of a war club. Swanton, *Social Organization,* p. 437.

[139] Bartram, *Travels,* p. 213.

[140] Bartram, *Travels,* pp. 488–489.

[141] Schoolcraft, V, p. 279.

[142] Swanton, *Social Organization,* p. 437.

[143] Swanton, *Social Organization,* p. 426.

[144] Speck, *Yuchi,* pp. 85, 116.

[145] Thomas, p. 676.

[146] Thomas, p. 675.

[147] Shetrone, p. 100.

gradual than in the Southeast and without the accompanying slavery. The explorations of the Cabots in 1494 and 1497 furnish practically no data on the Indians. The contacts made by Cartier on his three voyages to the St. Lawrence between 1534 and 1541 were essentially friendly and consequently the war practices and the treatment accorded captives by the Iroquois and Algonkians were not observed. Except for these slight contacts, the entire sixteenth century was a period of neglect of this part of the New World by the Europeans.

With the opening years of the seventeenth century the Algonkians and Iroquois of the region adjacent to the St. Lawrence quickly became familiar to the French Explorers and Missionaries. Champlain in 1603 and the succeeding years vividly describes the tortures of the Montagnais, Huron, Five Nation Iroquois, and even the Susquehanna of Pennsylvania in terms no different than those employed in the great number of cases cited in the Jesuit Relations all during the century. Death by torture was clearly a factor of extreme unpleasantness to be reckoned with in every contact with these northern Indians. The details varied somewhat from group to group but the following description of Huron treatment of one of the Five Nation Iroquois from Le Jeune's Relation of 1637 is reasonably typical of the tortures inflicted by Iroquoian speaking people of upper New York State and Canada:

Meanwhile the sun which was fast declining, admonished us to withdraw to the place where this cruel Tragedy was to be enacted. It was in the cabin of one Atsan, who is the great war Captain; Therefore it is called "Otinotsiskiaj ondaon," meaning, "the house of cut-off heads." It is there all the Councils of war are held; as to the house where the affairs of the country, and those which relate only to the observance of order, are transacted, it is called "Endionrra Ondaon," "house of the Council." . . . Towards 8 o'clock in the evening, eleven fires were lighted along the cabin, about one brass distant from each other. The people gathered immediately, the old men taking places above, upon a sort of platform, which extends, on both sides, the entire length of the cabin. The young men were below, but were so crowded that they were almost piled upon one another, so that there was hardly a passage along the fires. Cries of joy resounded on all sides; each provided himself, one with a firebrand, another with a piece of bark, to burn the victim. Before he was brought in, the Captain Aenons encouraged all to do their duty, representing to them the importance of this act, which was viewed, he said, by the Sun and by the God of war. He ordered that at first they should burn only his legs, so that he might hold out until daybreak; also for that night they were not to go and amuse themselves in the woods. He had hardly finished when the victim entered. I leave you to imagine the terror that seized him at the sight of these preparations. The cries redoubled at his arrival; he is made to sit down upon a mat, his hands are bound, then he rises and makes a tour of the cabin, singing and dancing; no one burns him this time, but also this is the limit of his rest—one can hardly tell what he will endure up to the time when they cut off his head. He had no sooner returned to his place than the war Captain took his robe and said, ''Oteiondi''—speaking of a Captain—''will despoil him of the robe which I hold''; and added, ''The Atachonchronons will cut off his head, which will be given to Ondessone, with one arm and the liver to make a feast.'' Behold his sentence thus pronounced. After this each one armed himself with a brand, or a piece of burning bark, and he began to walk, or rather to run, around the fires; each one struggled to burn him as he passed. Meanwhile, he shrieked like a lost soul; the whole crowd imitated his cries, or rather smothered them with horrible shouts. One must be there, to see a living picture of Hell. The whole cabin appeared as if on fire; and, althwart the flames and dense smoke that issued therefrom, these barbarians—crowding one upon the other, howling at the top of their voices, with firebrands in their hands, their eyes flashing with rage and fury—seemed like so many demons who would give no respite to this poor wretch. They often stopped him at the other end of the cabin, some of them taking his hands and breaking the bones thereof by sheer force; others pierced his ears with sticks which they left in them; others bound his wrists with cords which they tied roughly, pulling at each end of the cord with all their might. Did he make the round and pause for a little breath, he was made to repose upon hot ashes and burning coals. . . . But God permitted that on the seventh round of the cabin his strength should fail him. After he had reposed a short time upon the embers, they tried to make him rise as usual, but he did not stir; and one of these butchers having applied a brand to his loins, he was seized with a fainting fit, and would never have risen again if the young men had been permitted to have their way, for they had already begun to stir up the fire about him, as if to burn him. But the Captains prevented them from going any farther, and ordered them to cease tormenting him, saying it was important that he should see the daylight. They had him lifted upon a mat, most of the fires were extinguished, and many of the people went away. Now there was a little respite for our sufferer, and some consolation for us. . . . While he was in this condition, their only thought was to make him return to his senses, giving him many drinks composed of pure water only. At the end of an hour he began to revive a little, and to open his eyes; he was forthwith commanded to sing. He did this at first in a broken and, as it were, dying voice; but finally he sang so loud that he could be heard outside the cabin. The youth assembled again; they talk to him, they make him sit up—in a word they begin to act worse than before. For me to describe in detail all he endured during the rest of the night, would be almost impossible; we suffered enough in forcing ourselves to see a part of it. Of the rest we judged from their talk; and the smoke issuing from his roasted flesh revealed to us something of which we could not have borne the sight. One thing, in my opinion, greatly increased his consciousness of suffering —that anger and rage did not appear upon the faces of those who were tormenting him, but rather gentleness and humanity, their words expressing only raillery or tokens of friendship and goodwill. There was no strife as to who should burn him—each one took his turn; thus they gave themselves leisure to meditate some new devise to make him feel the fire more keenly. They hardly burned him anywhere except in the legs, but these, to be sure, they reduced to a wretched state, the flesh being all in shreds. Some applied burning brands to them and did not withdraw them until he uttered loud cries; and, as soon as he ceased shrieking, they again began to burn him, repeating it seven or eight times— often reviving the fire, which they held close against the flesh, by blowing upon it. Others bound cords around him and then set them on fire, thus burning him slowly and causing him the keenest agony. There were some who made him put his feet on red-hot hatchets, and then pressed down on them. You could have heard the flesh hiss, and seen the smoke which issued therefrom rise even to the roof of the cabin. They struck him with clubs upon the head, and passed small sticks through his ears; they broke the rest of his fingers; they stirred up the fire all around his feet. No one spared himself, and each one strove to surpass his companion in cruelty. But, as I have said, what was most calculated in all this to plunge him into despair, was their raillery, and the compliments they paid him when they approached to burn him. This one said to him, "Here, uncle, I must burn thee"; and afterwards this uncle found himself changed into a canoe. "Come," said he, "let us caulk and pitch my canoe, it is a beautiful new canoe which I lately traded for; I must stop all the water holes well," and meanwhile he was passing the brand all along his legs. Another one asked him, "Come, uncle, where do you prefer that I should burn you?" and this poor sufferer had to indicate some particular place. At this, another one came along and said, "For my part, I do not know anything about burning; it is a trade that I never practised," and meantime his actions were more cruel than those of the others. In the midst of this heat, there were some who tried to make him believe that he was cold. "Ah, it is not right," said one, "that my uncle should be cold; I must warm thee." Another one added, "Now as my uncle has kindly deigned to come and live among the Hurons, I must make him a present, I must give him a hatchet," and with that he jeeringly applied to his feet a red-hot hatchet. Another one likewise made him a pair of stockings from old rags, which he afterwards set on fire; and often, after having made him utter loud cries, he asked him, "And now, uncle, hast thou had enough?" And when he replied, "onnachouaten, onna," "Yes, nephew, it is enough, it is enough," these barbarians replied, "No, it is not enough," and continued to burn him at intervals, demanding of him every time if it was enough. They did not fail from time to time to give him something to eat, and to pour water into his mouth, to make him endure until morning; and you might have seen, at the same time, green ears of corn roasting at the fire and near them red-hot hatchets; and sometimes, almost at the same moment that they were giving him of the ears to eat, they were putting the hatchets upon his feet. If he refused to eat, "Indeed," said they, "dost thou think thou art master here?" and some added, "For my part, I believe thou wert the only Captain in thy country. But let us see, wert thou not very cruel to prisoners; now just tell us, didst thou not enjoy burning them? Thou didst not think thou wert to be treated in the same way, but perhaps thou didst think thou hadst killed all the Hurons?"

Behold in part how passed the night, ... One thing that consoled us was to see the patience which he bore all this pain. In the midst of their taunts and jeers, not one abusive or impatient word escaped his lips. . . . He himself also entertained the company for a while, on the state of affairs in his country, and the death of some Hurons who had been taken in war. He did this as easily, and with a countenance as composed, as anyone there present would have showed. This availed him at least as so much dimunition of his sufferings; therefore, he said, they were doing him a great favor by asking him many questions, and that this in some measure diverted him from his troubles. As soon as day began to dawn, they lighted fires outside the village, to display there the excess of their cruelty to the sight of the Sun. The victim was lead thither. . . . Meanwhile, two of them took hold of him and made him mount a scaffold 6 or 7 feet high; 3 or 4 of these barbarians followed him. They tied him to a tree which passed across it, but in such a way he was free to turn around. There they began to burn him more cruelly than ever, leaving no part of his body to which fire was not applied at intervals. When one of these butchers began to burn him and to crowd him closely, in trying to escape him, he fell into the hands of another who gave him no better reception. From time to time they were supplied with new brands, which they thrust, all aflame, down his throat, even forcing them into his fundament. They burned his eyes; they applied red-hot hatchets to his shoulders; they hung some around his neck, which they turned now upon his back, now upon his breast, according to the position he took in order to avoid the weight of this burden. If he attempted to sit or crouch down, someone thrust a brand from under the scaffolding which soon caused him to arise. . . . They so harassed him upon all sides that they finally put him out of breath; they poured water into his mouth to strengthen his heart, and the Captains called out to him that he should take a little breath. But he remained still, his mouth open, and almost motionless. Therefore, fearing that he would die otherwise than by the knife, one cut off a foot, another a hand, and almost at the same time a third severed the head from the shoulders, throwing it into the crowd, where someone caught it to carry it to the Captain Ondessone, for whom it had been reserved, in order to make a feast therewith. As for the trunk, it remained at Arontaen, where a feast was made of it the same day. . . . On the way (home) we encountered a Savage who was carrying upon a skewer one of his half-roasted hands.[148]

Captives were usually treated brutally from the moment of capture. The physical condition of the prisoner due to this abuse might be such that he was not acceptable for adoption.[149] At times, particularly if the captive had been tentatively assigned for adoption, there might be a period prior to torturing when he was treated handsomely and feasted.[150] A Shawnee captive of the Iroquois was said to have been unharmed from the time of capture and upon arrival in the village had not been greeted with blows but had been dressed and given to three women to replace a kinsman. Adoption had apparently been in the minds of the captors from the beginning, although in this case torture was finally inflicted upon the Shawnee.[151] An exception to these reports of initial harsh treatment is the remark by Colden that he knew of no case where the captive was offered the least abuse,[152] but this is undoubtedly an overstatement. The journey to the village of the captors might take some time, and it was customary to stop at each village passed and to force the captives to run between two lines of women and children, who beat them with clubs, to a platform where they were exhibited for the amusement and abuse of the inhabitants.[153]

Women seem to have rarely been tortured, but were rather kept to repopulate the villages decimated by constant warfare.[154] There may have been some tribal differences in this respect. The Neutrals were accused of torturing women in contrast to the Hurons who, supposedly, did not do so.[155] The Mohawks may have burned only the old women.[156] The Susquehanna were accused of burning a woman too injured to be of value as a captive.[157] The Onondaga apparently made little distinction between age and sex in their torture victims,[158] even torturing a boy of about ten years.[159] In 1667 the Oneida burned four Sus-

---

[148] *Jesuit Relations*, **13**, pp. 59–79.
[149] *Jesuit Relations*, **13**, pp. 39 f.
[150] *Jesuit Relations*, **13**, pp. 37; **42**, p. 177—Beauchamps, *A History*, p. 178.
[151] Galinee, p. 183.
[152] Schoolcraft, III, p. 188.
[153] *Jesuit Relations*, **39**, pp. 57, 175.
[154] Beauchamps, *A History*, pp. 196 f.
[155] *Jesuit Relations*, **21**, p. 195.
[156] Megapolensis, p. 174.
[157] *Jesuit Relations*, **42**, p. 189.
[158] *Jesuit Relations*, **47**, p. 147.
[159] *Jesuit Relations*, **42**, p. 189.

quehanna women,[160] and there are several other accounts of the
Five Nations torturing women.[161]　Father Joques gives a description of the sacrifice of a woman by the Mohawk.　She was
first burned and then thrown into the fire as an offering to the
war god Aireskoi to assure further victories over their enemies.
Pieces of this woman were then distributed to various villages
to be eaten in solemn feasts during the winter.[162]

The selection of victims for torture seems to have depended
largely upon their desirability for adoption.　According to one
of the earlier Relations, a council of old men determined the
disposal of all trophies of war, including the allocation of captives for adoption and the selection of the town in which the
others were to be burned.[163]　It has also been stated that the
uterine family through its matron decided the fate of the captive.[164]　However, should a captive be adopted either through
such assignment or by choice expressed by relatives of deceased
warriors [165] or by others,[166] and then prove unsatisfactory he
could still be given over to torture.[167]　Perhaps the most common
form of adoption was for a widow to replace a lost husband,[168]
but should this man prove unsatisfactory after adoption he might
be tortured.[169]　An Iroquois chief was reputed to have adopted
and subsequently burned 40 prisoners because they did not prove
worthy to succeed his dead brother.[170]　Another chief reputedly
tortured 80 captives to the shade of his brother.[171]　In 1669 an
old Seneca woman gave the captive alloted to her to replace her
dead son over to torture because she could not bear to see him
alive.[172]　So great was the power of a relative over the disposal
of a captive that the wishes of the tribe might be ignored even
in the face of a possible ensuing war.[173]

[160] Beauchamps, *A History*, p. 219.
[161] *Jesuit Relations*, 47, pp. 53–65, 35.
[162] *Jesuit Relations*, 39, pp. 219–221.
[163] *Jesuit Relations*, 13, p. 37.
[164] Hewitt, *The League of the Iroquois*, p. 533.
[165] Morgan, I, p. 333—*Jesuit Relations*, 13, p. 37 f.; 22, p. 259 f.; 31, p. 53; 42,
pp. 177, 191–195—Megapolensis, p. 179—Schoolcraft, III, p. 188—Galinee, p. 183.
[166] Morgan, I, p. 332.
[167] Morgan, I, p. 277—Schoolcraft, III, p. 189.
[168] *Jesuit Relations*, 42, p. 177—Beauchamps, *A History*, p. 199.
[169] *Jesuit Relations*, 42, pp. 177–179.
[170] *Jesuit Relations*, 42, pp. 191–195.
[171] *Jesuit Relations*, 48, p. 169.
[172] Galinee, p. 184.
[173] *Jesuit Relations*, 42, p. 177.

Formal torture seems to have fallen into two distinct parts. The first was enacted in a large cabin and lasted all night.[174] This cabin has been identified, in one case, as that of the war chief which was used for war councils.[175]   The victim was compelled to run around a row of fires while the young men applied brands and other forms of torture to him, reviving him when he fainted, and taking care not to cause his death, for it was essential that he last until dawn.[176]   It is probable that only men were present, the younger ones taking the more active role and the elders watching the proceedings.[177]   Any levity on the part of the participants, or going out into the woods for "amusement," was strictly prohibited, because the Sun and the God of War viewed the application of torture.[178]

At dawn the victim would be taken outside, where fires had been lighted, and forced to mount a platform 7 or 8 feet high. He was fastened loosely to this and tortured to death in front of the entire population.[179]   Torture on the platform might occur, however, without the earlier cabin torture.[180]   On one occasion, the Susquehanna made the victim mount the platform and then shoved him off into a fire, from which they rescued him, and contined to torture him.[181]   Relative freedom of movement, not binding to a stake, seems to have been the general rule. The Seneca once, after six hours of applying hot irons to the victim on the platform, compelled him to run through the village for two more hours, while they beat him with brands.[182]

The victim was expected to sing and dance at all times.   He did this when a farewell feast was given before torture began, in the case of his having been previously adopted, and in the cabin during the night of torture.[183]   Songs were largely boasting and emphasized the lack of fear on the part of the singer. On the return journey after capture, songs were required in each village visited, and upon arrival at the home village more were

174 *Jesuit Relations,* **13,** p. 59–22, p. 259—Murray, p. 75.
175 *Jesuit Relations,* **13,** p. 59.
176 *Jesuit Relations,* **13,** pp. 61, 65; **22,** p. 263.
177 *Jesuit Relations,* **13,** p. 61.
178 *Jesuit Relations,* **13,** p. 61; **17,** p. 159.
179 *Jesuit Relations,* **13,** p. 77; **22,** p. 263; **17,** p. 65.
180 *Jesuit Relations,* **45,** p. 257—Galinee, p. 184.
181 Lindestrom, p. 242.
182 Galinee, p. 186.
183 *Jesuit Relations,* **13,** p. 37 f.

insisted upon.[184] Songs were expected all during the torture.[185]
There is one account of an Algonkian who ate his own flesh,
which was fed to him by an Iroquois, without showing signs of
repugnance.[186] There is not enough evidence to show clearly the
attitude expected of the torturers to the bravery of the victim.
They seem to have expected him to sing, and forced him to do
so as much as possible. Bravery might be rewarded by a form
of heart or blood cannibalism. However, there are accounts
which suggest that it was considered an evil omen should no
pain be shown.[187] Such competition between the victim and the
torturers, the torturers being under urgent need to break the
spirit of the victim, appears to have been relatively rare. A
tradition of a Seneca warrior captured, tortured, and finally
escaping from the Choctaw, perhaps indicates the attitude expected by the Seneca of one of their own warriors in the hands
of the enemy. He boasted of feeling no pain, glorified his own
record for martial deeds, told them what the Seneca would do
in revenge, and sang his farewell song.[188]

The methods of torturing varied considerably and showed
quite a bit of ingenuity. Included among them were: applying
brands, embers, and hot metal to various parts of body; putting
hot sand and embers on scalped head; hanging hot hatchets about
neck; tearing out hair and beard; firing cords bound around
body; mutilating ears, nose, lips, eyes, tongue, and various parts
of the body; searing mutilated parts of the body; biting or tearing out nails; twisting fingers off; driving skewers in finger
stumps; pulling sinews out of arms; etc.[189] Mary Jemison mentions certain other methods which apparently did not appear
until after 1755, as they have not been noted in the earlier
sources. These included firing of pine splinters stuck in the
victim, and, in the case of Thomas Boyd, pulling out the intes-
tines.[190]

There seems to have been a definite feeling that death should

[184] *Jesuit Relations*, 22, p. 259; 39, p. 57.

[185] *Jesuit Relations*, 10, pp. 227–229; 39, pp. 57, 175; 4, p. 201—Megapolensis,
p. 174—Champlain, IV, p. 100.

[186] Champlain, V, p. 311.

[187] *Jesuit Relations*, 22, p. 259.

[188] The author is indebted to Dr. W. N. Fenton for this account.

[189] Some of the more complete descriptions of these methods are found in the
Jesuit Relations, I, pp. 271–273; 10, pp. 227–229; 13, pp. 37–79; 22, pp. 259–267;
39, pp. 57–77; etc.

[190] Seaver, pp. 37, 122.

not occur by fire or directly under torture. The sacrifice of the woman to the war god, previously noted, was an exception to this. Death by the knife was commonly required,[191] and likewise beating in the head of the victim.[192] Cutting off the head or limbs of the still living, but unconscious, victim is mentioned,[193] and the heart would sometimes be torn out before death.[194] The Susquehanna are mentioned as having released a tortured captive just before death, in order to allow the boys to shoot him while he attempted to run away.[195]

Cannibalism apparently invariably accompanied torture among all Iroquois speaking people. It was also most important to eat at solemn feasts the flesh of the woman sacrificed to the war god, and it is significant that the Iroquois made a feast of bear meat to the war god as atonement for not eating captives, and promised to do so in the future if success in war were granted.[196] "Eating" of the enemy was even used as a threatening expression.[197] The Mohawks were accused, by the Dutch, of eating slain enemies,[198] and the Iroquois supposedly ate war victims as late as 1756.[199] In addition to general cannibalism with every case of torture,[200] emphasis was placed particularly upon the heart, which might be torn from the still living victim, roasted and eaten.[201] The heart might be fed to the young men of the tribe,[202] or the captive might be forced to eat his own body or that of his comrades.[203] The blood might also be drunk,[204] or fed to children,[205] or put directly into the veins through a cut.[206] This seems to have been done only if the victim had been espe-

[191] *Jesuit Relations*, **13**, p. 79; **17**, p. 65.
[192] *Jesuit Relations*, **10**, pp. 227–229. Galinee, p. 186.
[193] *Jesuit Relations*, **10**, p. 227; **13**, pp. 61, 79.
[194] *Jesuit Relations*, **22**, p. 265; **34**, p. 27; I, p. 273.
[195] Lindestrom, p. 242.
[196] *Jesuit Relations*, **39**, pp. 219 f.—Megapolensis, p. 177.
[197] Tonty, *Memoir*, p. 57.
[198] Wassenaer, p. 84.
[199] Heckwelder, p. 54.
[200] *Jesuit Relations*, **4**, p. 201; **10**, pp. 227–229; **22**, pp. 253, 255, 259; **13**, pp. 79, 283; **39**, pp. 57, 81; **17**, p. 75—Megapolensis, p. 174—Galinee, p. 186—Murray, p. 75.
[201] *Jesuit Relations*, **22**, p. 259; **34**, p. 27.
[202] *Jesuit Relations*, **10**, pp. 227–229; I, p. 273.
[203] Champlain, IV, p. 100, V, p. 310—*Jesuit Relations*, **34**, p. 27—Hennepin, p. 198.
[204] *Jesuit Relations*, **34**, p. 27.
[205] Hennepin, p. 198.
[206] *Jesuit Relations*, **10**, pp. 227–229.

cially brave. A Dutch report states that the Mohawk reserved the head and heart for the chief, while the common people ate the trunk.[207] Just the opposite was averred for the Huron who, while normally presenting the head of game to the chief, as the choice morsel, gave the head of a human victim to the meanest person in the tribe.[208] However, another observer, a few years later, states that the head of the victim was given to the chief for a feast.[209] Le Jeune mentions an interesting form of cannibalism which has a curious resemblance to the Endo-cannibalism around the Gulf of Mexico. In the feast preparatory to war, a new-born child was shot with arrows, burned, and the ashes consumed.[210]

II. Torture Practices of Contiguous Groups

The Montagnais, as allies of the Huron, tortured captives taken from the Five Nations, employing the same methods as their reputed teachers, including cannibalism, but with perhaps more restrictions on the movements of the victim, less ceremonialism, and no use either of the preliminary torture in the large cabin or of a platform.[211] The Lenape usually adopted captives and torture was, according to Heckewelder, relatively rare and only done under extreme provocation from the Iroquois whom they accused of inventing the practice.[212] There does not seem to be any good evidence that torturing was indulged in by other Eastern Algonkians. It is, therefore, quite probable that neither the New England Algonkians nor those of Canada not in contact with the Iroquois practised torture as distinct from individual brutalities. After the arrival of the Iroquois in this region certain Algonkian tribes in direct conflict with them tortured from purely retaliatory motives. Flannery reaches a similar conclusion regarding Eastern Algonkian torture:

Lacking from Northern Algonkian. More probably due to Iroquois influence among the Coastal Algonkian.[213]

207 Megapolensis, p. 174.
208 Jesuit Relations, 10, p. 229.
209 Jesuit Relations, 13, pp. 61, 79.
210 Jesuit Relations, 19, p. 71.
211 Jesuit Relations, 5, pp. 27 f., 51 f.—Champlain, II, pp. 136 f., V, pp. 231 f.
212 Heckewelder, pp. 217 f., 343.
213 Flannery, p. 126.

Jenness attributed torture among the Indians of Canada entirely to the Iroquois.[214]

It is also probable that the Central Algonkians learned torturing from the Iroquois, and that it was not a trait of their culture prior to the Iroquois raids in the seventeenth century. The Illinois, who used approximately the same techniques, including eating the victim, as did the Iroquois, stated that they had learned from them, and did it only in retaliation.[215] Tonty was threatened with fire by the Tamaroas, an Illinois tribe, because he was mistaken for an Iroquois.[216] Penicaut credited them with killing captives with clubs and, therefore, as being less cruel than other tribes.[217] According to Bossu, referring to a later period, they burned Fox prisoners, and, in 1756, an Englishman brought back from Virginia.[218] The Ojibwa did not torture,[219] nor, apparently, did the Menomini[220] or the Sauk.[221] Forsyth reported that the Sauk and Fox treated enemies, if they did not kill them immediately, with the greatest humanity.[222] The Potawatomi seem to have tied those condemned by the council to a stake and shot them.[223] The Miami were accused of still burning captives as late as 1812, but the older practice is not clear. A Cannibalistic Society to which prisoners were given has been mentioned, but the mode of death is not stated.[224] The Shawnese Prophet told Trowbridge that he had seen the Kickapoo burn a white man about 1812. He had first been led into the village, painted black, and the next day tortured about three miles away from the village in a manner very similar to that described by Adair for the Chickasaw. His body was eaten by the torturers.[224a] This was a very late occurrence and was done in order to avenge the murder of a chief by the whites.

Torturing was certainly not characteristic of the Plains

214 Jenness, *Indians of Canada*, p. 279.
215 *Jesuit Relations*, 67, pp. 173 f.
216 Tonty, *Memoir*, p. 65.
217 Penicaut, p. 110.
218 Bossu, I, pp. 130, 186.
219 Jenness, *Indians of Canada*, p. 279.
220 Skinner, *War Customs*, p. 311.
221 Skinner, *Observations*, p. 72.
222 Blair, II, p. 97.
223 Skinner, *The Mascoutens*, pp. 40 f.
224 Trowbridge, pp. 23 f., 29.
224a Voegelin, pp. 20 f.

tribes. A recent study of the Plains war complex does not
refer to such behavior,[225] and a cursory examination of some of
the material pertaining to groups adjacent to the Woodlands
does not indicate that it was present in the cultures. The
Dakota were said to have sent captives home unharmed,[226] and,
according to Perrot, while they might tie them to stakes for the
boys to shoot, they never burned them except in reprisal against
the Iroquois.[227] Dorsey's source for mutilation of captives at
the stake by Dakota women is not given.[228] The Mandan [229] and
the Omaha [230] did not torture. Mrs. Kelly, a captive among the
Oglalla Sioux, writes of the horrible tortures which she not only
expected but which she actually went through, although, aside
from some death threats, there is no indication that she was
even particularly mistreated.[231] The Winnebago seldom took
prisoners unless for adoption, and an enemy not selected for
this was slain at once.[232] The Pawnee are accused by Dunbar
of delighting in tortures "like all Indians," but captives were
said to have been unusual and no specific details are furnished.[233]

The Quapaw, who should probably have been included among
the tribes of the lower Mississippi River, did torture those not
selected by the women for adoption. After compelling captives
to dance and sing, they were scalped and fastened to a frame
made of two posts and a crosspiece on which they were tor-
mented by the young people.[234] In 1706 they burned some
Hurons.[235]

The non-Caddoan tribes of Eastern Texas and the Gulf Coast
have been accused of torturing, but, except for the Karankawa,
no details are available. The Karankawa, according to the only
description found, seem to have had cannibalism of the still
living victim as the motivation for cruelty:

[225] Smith, Marian W.
[226] *Jesuit Relations,* 55, p. 181—Blair, I, p. 161, footnote.
[227] Blair, I, p. 169.
[228] Dorsey, *Omaha Sociology,* p. 313.
[229] Will and Spinden, p. 123.
[230] Dorsey, *Omaha Sociology,* p. 332—Fletcher, p. 603.
[231] Kelly.
[232] Schoolcraft, IV, p. 53.
[233] Dunbar, Par. 5.
[234] Bossu, I, pp. 105 f.
[235] Harpe, p. 35.

. . . they drive a big strong stake deep into the ground; to this they securely tie the unhappy prisoner; they build a log fire all around him; all of the rancheria, the tribe or confederation arrive, and when they sound the funeral instrument called a cayman, all begin to dance in a circle carrying in their hands well sharpened knives of iron (fierro) or flint, or a piece of shell. When they see fit they go up to the patient, cut off a piece of his flesh, pass it over the fire and dripping with blood, they eat it in sight of the victim, ... In this way they go on tearing the victim to pieces until he dies. . . . After they eat all of the flesh, they divide the bones among themselves, and those who are able to get a piece, go about continually gnawing and sucking it, until they consume it. Sometimes they hang the prisoner up by his feet, building a fire under him, let him roast, and then slowly eat him. Others make little pegs from the pine of which there is an abundance on the coast, and stick them into the body of the captive, set them on fire, and when they are burned off, eat the larded corpse.[236]

III. Summary of Torture Material

The material which has been presented seems to indicate that four patterns of torture can be defined within the region and that these were geographically delimited. They may be classified on the basis of the method of securing the victim as Frame torture among the tribes of the lower Mississippi River, Platform torture of the Northern Iroquois, Pole torture of the Chickasaw and Stake torture by several of the remaining groups. There is little descriptive data on Stake torture other than mere statements that the victim was tied to a stake and burned to death. As will be pointed out later, there is evidence to suggest that Pole and Stake torture probably do not represent distinct complexes. The following table defines the more significant differences between these torture patterns, certain aberrations being temporarily ignored. Other elements of interest in the torture complex are not subject to such comparative treatment but will be discussed separately.

[236] Morfi, pp. 51–52.

	Frame	Platform	Pole	Stake
Method of securing victim	Bound by wrists and ankles to frame	Free to move at all times	Fastened to pole with large radius of movement	Bound to a stake
Place of torture	In front of temple (?)	In cabin of War Chief all night. On platform outside at dawn	At last camp outside village	Within village or where convenient
Treatment prior to torture	Neither abused nor insulted	Continuously abused	Continuously abused	Continuously abused
Duration of torture	Up to several days	Many hours	Few hours	Moments (?)
Torture inflicted by:	Men only	Men in cabin, entire population on platform at dawn	Women only	Entire population (?)
Manner of death	Under torture	By knife or blow. Not under torture	Under torture	Consumed by fire
Scalping of victim	Before torture began	Part of torture	After death	
Cannibalism on victim	Lacking	Customary	Lacking	Lacking
Ceremonial elements	Ceremonial scalping. Touching with brands by captor. Dancing in front of temple. Lack of abuse. Use of frame. Inflicted by men only	Circumspect behavior by torturers. Dancing and singing of victim. Death on platform at sunrise. Death by knife or blow. Cardiac features. Cannibalism	Lacking	Lacking

IV. War Trophy Patterns

Torture was basically one method of disposing of war trophies, specifically captives. Scalps might also serve as trophies. Instead of being tortured, captives might be slain soon after seizure, kept as slaves, adopted into the tribe, serve as human sacrifice victims or be devoured, without any deliberate torture accompanying these acts. The different attitudes expressed by such a variety of behavior patterns were reflected in the treatment of scalps which might serve as sacrifice offerings, as a means of appeasing ghosts of slain warriors and closing the mourning period of relatives, or merely as symbols of bravery worn by the scalper. The act of torturing cannot be evaluated abstracted from its context in the total war trophy pattern and it will therefore be necessary to examine the related elements in order to clarify the behavior exhibited in the torture of captives.

An analysis of the available material, unquestionably scanty in many respect, indicates that three basically distinct patterns of behavior towards war trophies were exhibited in the region under consideration. These may be defined broadly as Old Southeastern, Intrusive Southeastern and Iroquois.

Old Southeastern Pattern

The tribes grouped under this pattern are the Southern Caddoans, Natchez, Taensa, Tunica, Koroa, Calusa, Timucua, Eastern Siouans, Southeastern Algonkians and Yuchi.

Scalps, or "Heads," seem to have been treated primarily as sacrificial offerings to the supernatural rather than for ghost appeasement or as badges of war prowess. The connections of scalp trophies with the temples emphasize this sacrificial attitude. After singing to the "heads" hung in trees the Hasinai buried them in the ashes of the perpetual fire maintained in the temple and offered food to them.[237] Scalps were also hung on poles during the dance prior to war [238] and were exhibited in front of the houses.[239] Food and tobacco were offered the scalps which were carried by the women in processions.[240] It is only in the Plains-like culture of the Wichita that scalps seem to have had the function of closing the mourning period.[241] The Pawnee used scalps ceremonially as offerings.[242]

This sacrificial attitude towards scalps and their connection with the temples was observed among the lower Mississippi River tribes as early as the time of De Soto:

[237] Hatcher, **31,** pp. 174, 217—Morfi, pp. 39, 40. Joutel may have seen temples as he remarked on the large separate huts used for ceremonies and public gatherings. Joutel, *Historical Journal,* p. 148 and *Relation,* p. 343.

[238] Hatcher, **30,** p. 124.

[239] Hatcher, **31,** p. 57.

[240] Joutel, *Historical Journal,* p. 161.

[241] Dorsey, George A., pp. 15–16.

[242] Dunbar, Par. 3.

. . . that they were going to cut their (Spaniard's) throats and put their heads upon lances at the entrances of the temples, ...[243]

Heads on lances at the doors of temples were also seen among the Pacaha [244] by the De Soto expedition,[245] and 150 years later around Taensa temples by Tonty.[246] In 1699 the Mongoulaches and Bayagoulas were reported by d'Iberville as decorating their temples with scalps.[247]

Although captives were desired as war trophies and 10 prisoners counted the same as 20 scalps towards the title of "Great Man Slayer," [248] scalps seems to have played the more significant part in the trophy pattern. The torture victim was ceremoniously scalped prior to torture.[249] Scalps, not captives, were the stated objective of a war party and were the trophy boasted about upon its return.[250] They seem to have been required for the privilege of tattooing the body.[251] After taking a scalp the warrior was compelled to submit to a period of continence and obey certain food taboos.[252] There is one reference to the use of scalps to dry the tears of relatives of slain warriors by the Natchez.[253]

Scalping was not reported for the Calusa of Florida but among the Timucua it was important.[254] If neither scalps nor captives were brought back as a sign of victory, an innocent Indian might be beaten to remind them that they must lament for past losses.[255] Scalps were immediately removed and carried home on lances where they were set up around the Chief's house, crowned with laurel, and became the center of the victory celebration.[256] This is suggestively similar to the Caddo and Natchez practices of associating scalps and temples. Old women carried the scalps in dances prasing the Sun for victory.[257]

[243] Vega, p. 457.
[244] Identified as Tunica by Swanton, *Relation of the Southeast*, pp. 62–63.
[245] Vega, p. 411.
[246] Tonty, *Memoir*, p. 61—*Jesuit Relations*, **68**, p. 125.
[247] Iberville, *Historical Journal*, p. 74.
[248] *Jesuit Relations*, **68**, p. 151.
[249] Du Pratz, II, p. 429.
[250] Du Pratz, II, pp. 421 f.
[251] Du Pratz, II, p. 199.
[252] *Jesuit Relations*, **68**, pp. 151–153—Charlevoix, *Historical Journal*, pp. 167 f.
[253] *Jesuit Relations*, **68**, p. 149—Charlevoix, *Historical Journal*, p. 167.
[254] Laudonnière, p. 413.
[255] Laudonnière, p. 462.
[256] Laudonnière, p. 464.
[257] Laudonnière, pp. 413–414.

Scalping may have been performed by special men appointed for the purpose who furthermore mutilated and burned the corpses.[258]   Scalps were set up on sticks along trails as a declaration of war.[259]   Before taking the war-path the Sun was asked for victory, and the women beseeched the leader to avenge the deaths of their husbands.[260]

Little is known of the Eastern Siouan trophy pattern.   Teeth as well as scalps were taken.[261]   A curious use of scalps, perhaps as a substitute for human sacrifice, was reported by Lederer in 1669 for the Watary:

. . . his (the King's) barbarous superstition, in hiring three youths, and sending them forth to kill as many young women of their enemies as they could light on, to serve his son, then newly dead, in the other world, as he vainly fancyed.   These youths during my stay returned with the skins torn off the heads and faces of three young girls, which they presented to his majestie, and were by him gratefully received.[262]

Scalping by the Southeastern Algonkians is not prominent in the accounts of the Jamestown colonists.   There is one reference to Powhatan ordering scalps hung on a line between trees near his cabin.[263]

The Yuchi in 1906 recalled that scalps had been carried stretched on hoops by the women relatives of the scalper in the victory celebration.[264]   No earlier descriptions have been found.

The evidence which has been presented strongly suggests that scalps were looked upon primarily as sacrificial offerings to supernatural beings by the groups included in the Old Southeastern Pattern.   It is perhaps significant that the Aztec likewise impaled the heads of sacrifice victims around the temples.[265]

It is difficult to distinguish slavery from adoption on the basis of some of the accounts but it is probable that true slavery did exist in the Southeast.   Captives with the tendons of their feet cut to prevent escape were seen by the De Soto expedition along the Mississippi.[266]   Lawson made a similar observation

[258] LeMoyne, p. 7.
[259] LeMoyne, p. 13.
[260] LeMoyne, p. 13.
[261] Lawson, p. 198.
[262] Lederer, p. 19.
[263] Strachey, p. 36.
[264] Speck, *Yuchi*, p. 85.
[265] Sahagun, pp. 61, 110.
[266] Vega, p. 419.

for Carolina 150 years later.[267]   The same method for restricting
the movements of slaves was employed by the Aztec.[268]   Slavery,
probably among Eastern Siouans, was noted as early as 1525.[269]

It is probable that the Calusa treated Fontaneda and other
shipwrecked Spaniards as slaves.   Cabeza de Vaca speaks of
his life in the vicinity of the Gulf Coast as slavery.   Ortis likewise appears to have been enslaved by the Indians of Florida.
The Timucua took men, women and children captive [270] but there
is no account of their final disposal except the statement of
Charlevoix that women and children were enslaved and men
sacrificed.[271]

Powhatan was said to have kept women and children, and
even chiefs, as captives but their exact status is not clear.[272]
However immediate death seems to have been more usual for all
enemies regardless of sex or age.[273]

Adoption as distinct from slavery is not mentioned for any
of the groups in this Old Southeastern Pattern with the possible
exception that a Natchez woman could perhaps demand a captive
to replace her husband.[274]   There is no indication that such
adoption was at all an important factor in the disposal of captives as most reports state that all men were tortured.[275]   There
are no accounts of either slavery or adoption among the Southern Caddoans although the related Wichita apparently had
slaves.[276]   Such negative evidence is not very conclusive.

Human sacrifice was an important element among the groups
included in the Old Southeastern Pattern.   Much of this sacrifice
did not involve captives directly or exclusively but included
relatives of a decreased person, children and slaves.

While the idea of offerings in the temples, including scalps,
was found among the Southern Caddoans, only one case of human sacrifice has been mentioned.   This involved the immola-
tion of children when a ''house'' was burned.[277]

[267] Lawson, p. 198.
[268] Bandelier, *On the Art of War*, p. 139.
[269] Martyr, II, p. 261.
[270] Laudonnière, pp. 464, 469.
[271] See p. 162.
[272] Smith, *A Map of Virginia*, p. 106—Strachey, p. 107.
[273] Smith, *The Generall Historie*, p. 358—Beverley, pp. 40, 150.
[274] Du Pratz, II, p. 432.
[275] Du Pratz, II, p. 428—Charlevoix, *Historical Journal*, p. 167—*Jesuit Rela-tions*, **68**, p. 149.
[276] Dorsey, George A., pp. 7, 13.
[277] Hatcher, **30**, p. 303.

On the lower Mississippi the extensive practice of human sacrifice was observed as early as the time of De Soto:

. . . commanded two young and well proportioned Indians to be brought thither; and said, that the use of the country was, when any lord died, to kill Indians to wait upon him and serve him by the way . . . and prayed Luys de Moscoso to command them to be beheaded. . . .[278]

An Indian boy, who had followed the Spaniards when they left Guachoia, said that he, being an orphan, had been adopted by the chief, but that:

. . . when his generous benefactor had taken sick and died, they chose him to be buried alive with him; because they said he was loved by him so much that he ought to accompany him to the other world in order to serve him there in his wants.[279]

Tonty noted the sacrifice of wives and retainers in 1681.[280] Ru, with d'Iberville in 1699, not only refers to Natchez sacrifices upon the death of a chief,[281] a practice which he also accuses the Taensa and Colapissa of indulging in, but in addition notes that they threw children into the fire because the temple had been struck by lightning.[282] This is confirmed by Penicaut.[283] Gravier mentions that children were sacrificed to appease a spirit made angry because no one had been slain on the death of the last chief.[284]

At the sacrifices upon the death of a Female Sun, scaffolds were erected to hold the bodies of the victims strangled by their relatives after they had danced in front of the temple.[285] Charlevoix states that the victims each mounted a separate scaffold in a public place from which they descended to dance in front of the temple from time to time. After three days each was strangled by relatives of the Woman Chief.[286] Families who sacrificed children might thus obtain the rank of nobility.[287]

There is no indication that captives were sacrificed except in so far as their position as slaves made this inevitable.

[278] Elvas, p. 192.
[279] Vega, p. 441.
[280] Tonty, *Memoir*, p. 61.
[281] Ru, pp. 35, 37.
[282] Ru, p. 41.
[283] Penicaut, *Annals*, p. 58.
[284] *Jesuit Relations*, **65**, p. 139.
[285] Penicaut, *Annals*, pp. 92 f.
[286] Charlevoix, *Historical Journal*, pp. 163 f.
[287] Du Pratz, III, p. 44—Dumont, I, p. 181—Mereness, p. 148.

The Calusa were noted for human sacrifice and captives were specifically allotted for this purpose:

The chief of the Caloosa immolated every years one person, usually a Christian, to the principle of evil, as a propitiating offering; . . . .[288]
. . . the cacique and his father had sacrificed (shipwrecked Christians) to their idols.[289]

Sacrifices were made upon the death of a leading person as well as to idols:

On the death of a child of a chief, his subjects sacrificed some of their sons and daughters to accompany it on its journey after death. On the death of the chief, his servants were killed. The Christian captives were annually offered up as food to the idols, who were said to feed upon their eyes, and a dance was performed with the head of the victim.[290]

Two Spaniards who had spent 15 years with the Calusa were brought to Laudonnière at St. Johns River in 1564:

Moreover they tolde me, that every year in the time of the harvest, this savage King sacrificed one man, which was kept expressly for this purpose, and taken out of the number of the Spanyards which by tempest were cast upon that coast.[291]

Ortis was twice threatened with death by the Indians of Florida. One of these threats may possibly have involved torture and not human sacrifice [292] although the context is not clear. The second time sacrifice was definitely the motive:

These people being worshippers of the devil, are wont to offer up unto him lives and blood of their Indians, or of any other people they can come by; and they report that when he will have them do sacrifice unto him, he speaketh with them, and telleth them that he is athirst, and willeth them to sacrifice unto him.[293]

The sacrifice of children on the death of a King, probably by the Timucua, is mentioned by LeMoyne, as well as a curious sacrifice of a stuffed deerskin to the sun.[294] The sacrifice of prisoners to the sun by the Indians of Florida is referred to by Charlevoix whose information is perhaps based upon the above accounts.[295]

[288] Brinton, p. 94—citing Barcia.
[289] Lowery, 1905, p. 229.
[290] Lowery, 1905, p. 230—Swanton, *Early History*, p. 389.
[291] Laudonnière, p. 482.
[292] See p. 158.
[293] Elvas, p. 126.
[294] LeMoyne, p. 13.
[295] See p. 162.

The sacrifice of scalps to accompany the body of a deceased warrior among the Eastern Siouans [296] was perhaps a substitute for actual human sacrifice. Likewise Lawson's observation previously cited, that they believed the "Devil" would send a calamity if captives were not tortured implies a human sacrifice attitude towards torturing. Lederer's reference to human sacrifice on the death of a great man among the Indians of western Carolina and Virginia probably applies to the Siouans:

When their great men die, they likewise slay prisoners of war to attend them.[297]

There are several accounts of the sacrifice of children or strangers to a supernatural being by the Southeastern Algonkians.[298] One description of "sacrifice" was probably nothing more than an initiation ceremony involving feigned death by clubbing.[299]

Lederer's rather vague reference to the Oustack sacrificing enemies to their idols is the only early account of Yuchi human sacrifice.[300] In 1906 an informant told Speck that Yuchi captives were not only tortured in the square grounds but were also kept to serve as a sacrifice to the sun.[301]

Cannibalism does not seem to have been a practice of any of the tribes with the exception of the Southern Caddoans. Charlevoix does mention that men sacrificed to the sun were eaten [302] but his authority for the statement is not clear. Although cannibalism was charged against the Chichimecos [303] as early as 1675 [304] the source is very questionable in that the evidence was in the nature of a rumor about unknown "heathen" Indians outside the borders of Florida. Aside from such doubtful cases there seems to be little basis for assuming any cannibalism among the tribes of the lower Mississippi River or eastwards, and there is specific denial by Vega that the Indians of Florida practised it.[305] There are, however, several descriptions

[296] See p. 197.
[297] Lederer, p. 8.
[298] Strachey, p. 83—Spelman, pp. cv–cvl.
[299] Smith, *A Map of Virginia*, pp. 111–112—Strachey, pp. 93–94.
[300] Lederer, p. 21.
[301] Speck, *Yuchi*, pp. 85, 116.
[302] See p. 162.
[303] Identified by Swanton as Yuchi, Wenhold, p. 4.
[304] Wenhold, p. 11.
[305] Vega, p. 242.

of voracious cannibalism among the Southern Caddoans, and the brutalities practised on captives [306] seem to have been rather a prelude to cannibalism than true torture. Joutel states that the woman brutally killed was served up to two boys of her nation and that they also ate dried tongues of their enemies.[307] The non-Caddoan tribes of eastern Texas and the Gulf coast were undoubtedly voracious cannibals and it is possible that the Southern Caddoans learned the usage after coming into contact with them, perhaps due to a movement out of the southeast.

There is little to suggest that torture was a part of the war trophy pattern of the tribes along the Atlantic seaboard. As has been indicated in an earlier part of this study, no references to torturing have been noted in this region until almost 200 years after white contact. Furthermore, it seems even more significant that there are no expressions by the early explorers and colonizers indicating any fear of such treatment. The Europeans were only too willing in most cases to call attention to the barbarity of the Indians, and thus justify their need for either salvation or extermination. This is, of course, negative evidence for the most part, although there are several specific denials of torture, but the situation is striking in contrast to the terror inspired at the time of the first White-Iroquois relations in Canada. One possible exception to the absence of torture in this region of the southeast might be the treatment of Ortis. Details are lacking, and he may well have been threatened the first time, as he was later, with human sacrifice without torture, a practice undoubtedly present among the Timucua. The few incidents of burning at the stake, referred to long after the early Spanish contacts, were in the form so well known in Europe, which had been used on the Indians by De Soto, and undoubtedly by many others. It is not difficult to believe that the Indians would learn to retaliate in kind. The Saponi torture described by Lawson in the early eighteenth century was not European in type, but was very like that of the Iroquois with whom the Carolina Siouans were in contact at that time. The probability that neither Siouan nor Algonkian speaking peoples tortured except as retaliation against the Iroquois lends weight to the suggestion that it was absent among the Siouan and Algonkian tribes of the Southeastern Area. The evidence seems

[306] See p. 168.
[307] Joutel, *Historical Journal*, p. 161 and *Relation*, p. 380.

to be quite conclusive that none of the tribes along the Eastern Seaboard tortured captives until long after white contact, and when it finally appeared it was in retaliation against similar treatment at the hands of the whites or the Iroquois.

In the lower Mississippi region, captive torture had many ceremonial aspects, and was strongly oriented towards religion. Dancing in front of the temple by the victim was one feature of this ritual connection, a practice required of certain sacrificial victims by the Aztec.[308] Likewise respect shown to the victim before torture began, torture probably inflicted in front of the temple, participation by men only, and the ceremonial touching with a brand seem to indicate that torture had an important religious significance. Attachment of the victim to a frame was unique in the Southeast and this, coupled with the ceremonial application of the brand, perhaps suggests Mexican and Pawnee contacts.[309] Whether or not the Pawnee could have obtained the frame from the Natchez is beyond the scope of this paper. Other Caddoan tribes apparently lacked it. The parallels between Pawnee Morning Star Sacrifice traits and the Natchez torture practices are not impressive. The resemblances of the Natchez practice to that of the Mexican sacrifice to a war god or the sun are likewise not strikingly close, but seem slightly more cogent than the other. Natchez torture was of a man, and the association with the temple indicated sacrificial motivations. The frames were nearly identical, but the possibility for variations in these is not great. Otherwise there are few similarities. Cardiac features, cannibalism, and the use of the flayed skin of the victim were not associated with the Natchez torture, nor was death under agonies comparable to being shot by arrows. Nevertheless, the basic concept of men being sacrificed to a god may well have been of common origin, and the possible historical connection cannot be ignored. It is also somewhat significant chronologically, for if the Aztecs only received this ceremony of frame sacrifice in 1506 it is quite possible that it would not have reached the Mississippi until after the time of De Soto.[310] His failure to note torture, although he did find human sacrifice of a different sort, is not very reliable negative evidence, however. The supposition has been advanced that the late mention

308 Sahugun, p. 43.
309 Linton, p. 463.
310 See Wissler and Spinden, and Linton.

of Natchez torture indicates that it was acquired as a retaliatory measure against the Iroquois.[311]　There seems to be no adequate grounds for such an hypothesis.　A review of the material shows practically no similarity between the two torture complexes, but many striking differences.　Perhaps more pertinent evidence for the late appearance of Natchez torture is that it does not seem to have spread to the neighboring Choctaw and Chickasaw.

Except for the brutal killing of a woman captive by the women of the tribe, an act which bore little resemblance to institutionalized torturing, the Southern Caddo treatment of captives seems to have been cannibalism, with the infliction of pain as merely an incidental accompaniment.

To summarize in broad terms, it may be said that there is evidence for an older culture in the Southeast extending from eastern Texas to the Atlantic seaboard with a war trophy complex, including related traits, which had as a basis:

Scalps as offerings to the supernatural, not associated with mourning or ghosts.

Temples closely connected with warfare.

Human sacrifice to accompany the dead, or propitiate the supernatural, but only incidentally related to warfare or captives.

Slavery, not adoption, for war captives.

Torturing absent, excluding late development in retaliation against White and Iroquois, except on the lower Mississippi where it had religious motivations and may have been of relatively late origin.

Cannibalism absent, except among the Southern Caddoans, where a late diffusion from the surrounding tribes is indicated.

Swanton has remarked on similarities between the Atlantic Coast and the lower Mississippi region, in contrast to the intervening area, which:

. . . suggests rather strongly that the Creeks were comparatively late intruders into the section where they were found by the Europeans and that, in the process of settling there, they had displaced some cultural features which formerly extended unbrokenly from the Atlantic Ocean to the Mississippi.[312]

[311] Blair, I, 169, footnote.
[312] Swanton, *Aboriginal Culture of the Southeast*, p. 718.　See also p. 726.

Some of the traits taken to illustrate this were the use of ossu-aries, artificial head deformation, use of poison to destroy ene-mies, matrilinear descent without clans, and human sacrifice.[313] Other traits could undoubtedly be included, such as absence of mother-in-law taboo and a developed nobility with considerable power in the hands of the chiefs.[314]

The data on the war trophy patterns of the Atlantic Coast and lower Mississippi regions seem to confirm the underlying unity of an older widespread culture in the Gulf region of North America suggested by these parallels. It is perhaps identifiable with the early Proto-Muskhogean of Bushnell which grew out of a Yuchi-Siouan culture, and was basic to that of the Natchez, Timucua, and Calusa.[315] The unity of this culture is also indi-cated by pottery similarities between early Caddo, Moundsville of Alabama, Etowah of Georgia, and the northern Gulf Coast of Florida.[316] The pottery of east-central Texas has been con-sidered more like that of the Gulf Coast of Florida than of the closer Coast of Texas.[317]

In addition to the tribes which have been specifically included, the Choctaw should perhaps be added instead of being placed in the Intrusive Southeastern Pattern. The information is not complete enough on their war trophy patterns to indicate clearly their position. Other groups, such as the Chitimacha, were undoubtedly part of this older culture but their war patterns are practically unknown.

Intrusive Southeastern Pattern

Into this underlying widespread culture in the Southeast intrusions of other people with entirely distinct attitudes to-wards war trophies occurred. These later arrivals may be roughly identified as the Muskhogean Proper, although the exact tribal conformation is confused. The infiltration of Choctaw, Chickasaw, and Creek may have been gradual and accompanied by a considerable amount of fusion with the earlier culture. It is quite possible that the distinctive character of the new culture was due to the Creeks alone.

[313] Swanton, *Aboriginal Culture of the Southeast*, p. 718.
[314] Swanton, *Aboriginal Culture of the Southeast*, pp. 696, 700.
[315] Bushnell, *Tribal Migrations*.
[316] Stirling, p. 21.
[317] Pearce, p. 55.

. . . the Creeks, who are believed to have entered the region in very
late times, but the de Soto narratives show us that in the early 16th.
century part of the Creeks did not conform to this pattern. I am therefore inclined to attribute the standardization of Creek culture to a Creek
tribe which arrived from the northwest at a late period, ...[318]

The earliest reference to scalping by these tribes is that the
Apalachee prized the scalps of De Soto's followers to hang upon
their bows.[319] In 1559 the members of the de Luna expedition
saw a pole about fifteen feet high full of scalps standing in the
center of the square of a Napochies (Choctaw) village.[320]
Scalps rather than captives seem to have been the significant
trophy of war and even in the case of a tortured captive the
scalp was carefully protected and used later in the victory ceremony held in the town square.[321] Whole scalps were not necessary. One cut up into many pieces would suffice as a trophy
for the entire war party and enable each warrior to advance in
rank.[322] A scalp shared with a nephew or child, who was compelled to sing under the blows of the donor, gave him recognition as a warrior.[323] Scalps varied in value and their relative
merits were pronounced by the chief.[324] So important was the
scalp that the Creeks were accused of killing members of their
own tribe to obtain the necessary trophy,[325] and to prevent their
own scalps from falling into the hands of the enemy they scalped
their own dead.[326] Ghosts of slain warriors who had either lost
their scalps or had remained unburied were refused admission
to the "Mansions of Bliss" until surviving friends retaliated
upon the enemy.[327] This relationship between scalps and ghosts
was characteristic of all the tribes. They might be placed upon
the houses of the relatives of those slain without being
avenged,[328] on poles near the houses [329] or on the top of the
ceremonial sweathouse.[330] The souls of slain warriors were

318 Swanton, *Relation of the Southeast,* pp. 64–65.
319 Ranjel, p. 152.
320 Swanton, *Early History,* p. 236—citing Davila Padila.
321 Adair, p. 397.
322 Adair, pp. 167, 298, 388, 397—Schoolcraft, V, pp. 297 f.—Hawkins, *Sketch,*
p. 70.
323 Swanton, *An Early Account,* p. 66.
324 Milfort, pp. 249–250.
325 Adair, pp. 258–259.
326 Milfort, p. 253—Adair, p. 387—Dumont, p. 46.
327 Pope, pp. 63–64.
328 Adair, pp. 167, 397.
329 Cushman, p. 254.
330 Romans, p. 75.

supposed to haunt the eaves of their former dwellings [331] and not to leave until the scalps were placed there.[332] A report for the Choctaw states that all war booty, which probably included scalps, was given to relatives of deceased warriors to dry their tears.[333]

The ultimate disposal of the scalps is not clear. Undoubtedly they were often kept permanently on the poles or houses.[334] There are some references to their use in ceremonies.[335] They were sometimes worn as a headdress during the Busk ceremony at which time there was ceremonial scalping of effigies.[336] An informant told Swanton that the Alabama had buried a scalp under the ceremonial ball post.[337]

The religious attitude expressed by the emphasis upon the connection between scalps and ghosts is further brought out in the requirement of ritual purity on the part of the warriors. This involved sweating, fasting and drinking the emetic, or Black Drink, both before and after war.[338] Such ritual purity was even practised by Creeks during the civil war.[339] The insistence upon continence during the war period protected captured women from violation.[340] Another use of the Black Drink in association with mourning was observed by Ru in 1669. He noticed that Houma women drank water mixed with herbs and attempted to spew it up as part of the mourning ritual.[341] War was definitely connected with the idea of pollution and failure of a war party was blamed upon the impurity of the leader or some member of the party, or even upon those who had stayed at home.[342] "Holy" men were forbidden to slay and no warrior could officiate at religious ceremonies.[343] However, to counter-

---

[331] Schoolcraft, I, p. 210.

[332] Adair, p. 151.

[333] Bossu, I, pp. 294 f.

[334] Bartram, *Observations*, p. 35—Schoolcraft, V, p. 265.

[335] Adair, pp. 310, 421.

[336] Swanton, *Religious Beliefs*, p. 567 (citing Stiggins MS.)—pp. 572 f. (citing Hitchcock MS.).

[337] Swanton, *Religious Beliefs*, p. 544.

[338] Bossu, I, pp. 298 f.—Adair, pp. 119, 160, 166, 167—Milfort, pp. 238 f.— Hawkins, *Sketch*, p. 79—Speck, *Taskigi*, pp. 109, 118—Schoolcraft, V, pp. 538, 543, 265.

[339] Swanton, *Social Organization*, p. 436.

[340] Adair, p. 164—Schoolcraft, V, p. 272.

[341] Ru, pp. 28–29.

[342] Adair, pp. 163, 164, 166, 382, 416, 421 f.

[343] Adair, p. 152.

act impurity contracted by attacking women in their menstrual lodges, special herbs were carried.[344]

Except for one reference to eating the heart of a brave enemy, cannibalism is denied for these tribes.[345] Mutilations of the dead in addition to scalping did occur [346] but seem rather to have been a form of insult, similar to sodomy on a dead enemy,[347] with no cannibalistic connotations.

The placating of ghosts by the presentation of scalps was quite distinct from the idea of using the trophies as offerings to the supernatural at the temples found in the Old Southeastern Pattern. Consistent with this difference was the absence of temples and of any form of human sacrifice among these tribes. The satisfaction of the religious demands through the taking of scalps led to social advancement. Titles and war honors depended upon them [348] and they were about the only way in which such recognition could be obtained.

The emphasis upon scalps seems to have inhibited the enslavement or adoption of captives for the religious obligations required the scalp itself and could not be satisfied by captives. There was probably a certain amount of adoption [349] but it seems never to have reached sizeable proportions. The Choctaw were said to have "enslaved" women and children [350] but the connotations are not clear. This relatively slight weight attached to captives was of course changed by the introduction of the white man's slave complex.

There is strong probability that torture was not originally a part of this culture. As in the case of the Atlantic Coast tribes, there is no indication of torture until almost 200 years after European contact, and fear of such treatment from the Creeks was apparently entirely foreign to the early whites. Even at a late date, the evidence for the practice of torture is extremely scanty. Both Bartram and Milfort report that it had once been customary, but do not elaborate further. It is unfortunate that there is not more information on the torture at the slave posts, merely mentioned by Bartram. The reports

[344] Adair, p. 124.
[345] Adair, p. 135.
[346] Romans, p. 75—Adair, p. 37.
[347] Romans, p. 70.
[348] Adair, pp. 147, 151, 193—Bossu, II, p. 42.
[349] Adair, p. 154.
[350] Swanton, *An Early Account,* p. 66.

on the Yamassee torturing Spaniards and English in 1715 are very sketchy. These acts were apparently retaliatory in nature. Burning captives at the stake by the Apalachee in 1704 and by the Chickasaw in 1736 were typically European in pattern. Only the single account of Adair for the Chickasaw is reasonably complete, and there is much in it to indicate that torture was not integrated with the rest of the culture, but that the scalp was the dominant motive in the war trophy complex. The victim was turned over to the women to torture upon the return of the war party. There is no suggestion that he was presented to any one specifically with the idea of replacing slain relatives or satisfying mourners. He was beaten and tortured outside the village, and before the victory ceremonies were held in the square grounds within the village. The scalp of the victim, carefully protected during the tortures, was an important element in the later ceremonies. The entire act of torture apparently had no ceremonial connotations. The captive was not expected to dance or sing at any time, and seems to have had no function in satisfying religious emotions or in providing social recognition for his captor.

This particular Chickasaw torture complex has been distinguished from the stake torture on the basis of method of securing the victim and the kind of torments employed. The underlying attitude of pure retaliation without ceremonial elements would however indicate that it had much the same basis as stake torture with perhaps the addition of a certain amount of ingenuity possibly learned at this relatively late date from the Iroquois.

Most descriptions of torture definitely suggest the white pattern of burning at the stake. Retaliation as a motive appears to be prominent in the few cases of torturing by the Muskhogean Proper which have been recorded. The evidence seems quite conclusive that torture in this culture was a late development originating as a result of white, and perhaps some Iroquois, contacts. It is possible that burning captives as a retaliation against whites was sometimes fitted into the scalp complex for an old Spanish resident of Florida told Bartram that the Indians had formerly burned Spaniards to appease the spirits of slain relatives.[351]

[351] Bartram, *Travels*, p. 489.

The entire war complex of the Muskhogeans strongly suggests the Plains in many particulars. This is especially true
of the great emphasis upon the scalp in connection with mourning, a function of much significance in Plains warfare.[352] Such
elements as purification, absence of torture and cannibalism, and
the relatively few captives taken also resemble the Plains pattern, and lend additional weight to Swanton's conclusions on the
movements of the Muskhogeans based upon other evidence:

It is evident that the culture of the central region (of the Southeast) had
been markedly modified by influences and probably invasion from the
northwest.[353]

The Natchez may well have taken over the idea of using
scalps to dry the tears of mourners from these tribes, particularly the Choctaw, and added it to the older pattern in which
the significance of scalps was in their importance as offerings
to the supernatural. Purification may have been closely identified with the scalp relationship to the dead and been taken over
simultaneously by the Natchez. It is not, of course, yet clear
that the Choctaw were not a part of the older culture who were
more influenced by the intrusive culture than were the Natchez.

Iroquois Pattern

The third distinctive trophy pattern appeared among the
Northern Iroquois. Scalping was a feature of Iroquois warfare but not perhaps as significant as it was farther south where
Friederici placed its origin.[354] Scalps do not seem to have had
any connection with the souls of the dead warriors or to have
been given to their relatives. Perhaps an exception to this is
furnished in the account of Mary Jemison for the period after
1755 where the Seneca are said to have given scalps to mourners to dry their tears if no captives were available.[355] Furthermore the idea of scalps as offerings to the supernatural is likewise lacking.

Scalps seem to have been prized rather as badges of merit,
a sort of proof of valor, without any further connotations. The
scalper was evidently not permitted to make several out of one

[352] Smith, M. B., pp. 452 f.
[353] Swanton, *Southeastern Indians*, p. 20.
[354] Friederici, p. 428.
[355] Seaver, pp. 59–60.

by cutting them up, and he was esteemed for the number he could show, which implies that they were not given away.[356]   Scalps were painted and carried on poles,[357] and might serve to indicate the number of slain enemies to the village upon the return of the war party.[358]   A report of 1634 states that the Oneida put the scalps on Images carved like men on top of the gate to their village.[359]   Scalps were carried in preparatory war dances and in the victory celebrations, and a post was "scalped" by each warrior before setting out on the war-path.[360]   The torture victim might be scalped as a part of the brutality and without any deeper significance.[361]

There are practically no references to trophies of war other than scalps and captives.   An early Dutch account speaks of the Mohawk carrying home leg and arm bones,[362] and a Jesuit in 1626 noted heads being carried home.[363]   At late as 1776 the Wyandots and Migoes in Ohio were supposedly seen putting a head on a post and dancing around it.[364]

Captives rather than scalps were the more desirable war trophy and except for a relatively small number who were tortured they were adopted by relatives of slain warriors as a means of appeasing the dead.   A vivid picture of a substitution is furnished by the case of Father Poncet who had been captured by the Mohawk in 1653 and allotted to a widow for adoption:

So soon as I entered her cabin, she began to sing the song of the dead, in which she was joined by her two draughters. . . . and then I was in the place of the dead, for whom these women renewed the last mourning, to bring the deceased to life again in my person, according to their custom.[365]

A captive might be given to a relative of a deceased person although not necessarily of the same sex.   The thirteen-year-old

[356] Heckewelder, p. 216.
[357] *Jesuit Relations*, 39, p. 57; 53, pp. 145–147—Zeisberger, p. 105—Heckewelder, p. 216.
[358] Schoolcraft, III, p. 188.
[359] Unknown, p. 148.
[360] Heckewelder, pp. 209 f.
[361] *Jesuit Relations*, 17, p. 65; 22, p. 259; 34, p. 27—Champlain, IV, p. 100—Lindestrom, p. 242.
[362] Wassenaer, p. 85.
[363] *Jesuit Relations*, 4, p. 201.
[364] Leeth, p. 38.
[365] Beauchamps, *A History,* p. 199.

Mary Jemison was adopted by two Seneca women to replace a dead brother, for they considered her as sent by him to stand in his place and help them.[366] The relatives of slain warriors might even originate a war party by offering presents to someone to organize one.[367]

The policy of adopting individuals and even entire tribes to repopulate villages [368] carried the idea considerably further than any other group in eastern North America:

It was not confined to captives alone, but was extended to fragments of dismembered tribes, and even to the admission of independent nations into the League.[369]

After adoption the captives were treated as Iroquois in full standing. Colden expresses this policy as follows:

It has been a constant Maxim with the Five Nations, to save the Children and Young Men of the People they Conquer, to adopt them into their own Nation, and to educate them as their own Children.[370]

Should the adopted persons be unhappy it was possible to return home,[371] but usually they would be content to consider themselves as true Iroquois.[372] Morgan's conclusion that prisoners were virtually slaves for years does not seem to be substantiated by the data available.[373]

However, allocation for adoption to replace a deceased relative did not necessarily mean escape, for, as has been indicated under the discussion of torturing, many such individuals were later given over to tortures.[374] Also it was necessary for the candidate for adoption to have his hardihood tested by running the gauntlet, an act which has been referred to by Morgan as the adoption ceremony. Only those reaching the house of their adoptors by running through lines of people armed with clubs were saved. Those who fell were instantly slain.[375] These houses were not refuge places in the same sense as found among the Creeks. There is one doubtful allusion to a refuge town.[376]

[366] Seaver, pp. 57 f.
[367] *Jesuit Relations*, 16, p. 205; 10, pp. 227 f.
[368] *Jesuit Relations*, 43, p. 267.
[369] Morgan, I, p. 332.
[370] Colden, p. 110.
[371] Morgan, I, p. 332.
[372] Morgan, II, p. 277.
[373] Morgan, II, pp. 277 f.
[374] See p. 186.
[375] Morgan, I, pp. 333, 334. Hewitt, *The League of the Iroquois*, p. 342.
[376] Mooney, *Myths*, p. 208.

Many of the Iroquois war trophy practices were characteristic of the surrounding Algonkians. The Pottawatomi and Ottawas,[377] and the Sauk and Fox [378] extensively adopted captives to replace the deceased, as did the Lenape and other Eastern Algonkians. The Dakota Sioux did likewise in the case of Hennepin,[379] and the Winnebago [380] and Kansa [381] had a similar practice. The Iroquois adoption pattern seems to have been a widespread trait shared by the Algonkians and western Siouans but not significant in the Southeast. Running the gauntlet upon arrival at the village was in the nature of a test of the virtues of the captive preliminary to adoption and, like adoption, the Iroquois practice was characteristic of the Algonkians and Siouans but absent in the Southeast.

The great fear in which the Iroquois were held by their enemies was undoubtedly due in large part to the likelihood of being tortured if captured, and in this sense torture acted as an incentive towards submission. Its use to spread terror may have been a secondary development which was, nevertheless, consciously utilized, but there is much to indicate that human sacrifice was the underlying motivation. The woman burned and eaten as an offering to the war god was definitely such an act.[382] In many cases of the more customary torture of men the sacrificial motivation was indicated by the insistence on circumspect behavior on the part of the torturers, the dancing and singing required of the victim, kindness to and feasting of the victim, the requirement that death should occur only upon the platform at sunrise, death by a knife, cardiac features, and cannibalism. The feast of bear meat with the accompanying apology to the war god for not having tortured and eaten captives is an excellent illustration of this motive. Most of the above features were associated more or less completely with all torturing and strongly suggest that, while lust for vengeance and the spreading of terror may have become an important element, the concept of a sacrificial offering underlay the act, a possibility mentioned by Linton.[383] This type of human sacrifice, however, would seem to have little in common with that of the Southeastern groups

[377] Blair, II, p. 162.
[378] Blair, II, p. 197.
[379] Hennepin, pp. 210–211.
[380] Schoolcraft, IV, p. 53.
[381] Hunter, p. 328.
[382] See p. 186.
[383] Linton, p. 462.

either at the death of a chief or periodically to propitiate the supernatural.

Cases have been mentioned in which the life of a dog could be taken in lieu of that of a man, and it has been suggested by some that the White Dog Sacrifice was a late substitution for human sacrifice.[384] The ceremonial significance of the dog in Iroquois culture was closely associated with war. An interesting substitution is mentioned in one of the earlier Relations. A man, being tortured by his friends in order to fulfill a dream, substituted a dog, which was killed, burned, and eaten, "just as were captives."[385] Other animals might be similarly sacrificed.[386] Dogs were eaten in the feasts preparatory to going to war,[387] and in the adoption feast of a captive.[388] A "madman" in search of a man's head, and threatening a missionary, was persuaded to substitute that of a dog.[389] The White Dog Sacrifice in the mid-winter ceremonies was observed in the seventeenth century. These dogs were strangled on the first day of the ceremonies, and burned and eaten about the fifth day, after being decorated to represent a god.[390] The sacrifice of a dog, with the subsequent eating of it, was a part of the curing ceremony.[391]

The ceremonial importance of eating dog flesh at the feast preparatory to war had a wide distribution. It has been mentioned for the Natchez[392] and likewise occurred among the Abnaki,[393] Menomini,[394] Ojibwa,[395] Winnebagoes,[396] Oglalla,[397] Quapaw[398] and in Mexico.[399] The Micmacs sacrificed dogs as a part of the mourning ceremony.[400] There does not seem to be any particular reason why the ceremonial connotations attached to the dog

[384] Beauchamps, *A History*, pp. 131 f.
[385] *Jesuit Relations*, 23,, pp. 172–173.
[386] *Jesuit Relations*, 13, p. 159.
[387] *Jesuit Relations*, 9, p. 113.
[388] *Jesuit Relations*, 42, p. 191; 13, pp. 43 f.
[389] *Jesuit Relations*, 42, p. 43.
[390] Hewitt, *White Dog Sacrifice*, pp. 940, 943—Fenton, pp. 7, 11.
[391] *Jesuit Relations*, 13, p. 31; 57, p. 147.
[392] Du Pratz, II, pp. 421 f.
[393] *Jesuit Relations*, 67, p. 205.
[394] Skinner, *War Customs*, p. 306.
[395] Jenness, *Ojibwa Indians*, p. 102.
[396] Schoolcraft, IV, p. 52.
[397] Kelly, pp. 197 f.
[398] Bossu, I, p. 99 f.
[399] Sahagun, pp. 58, 177.
[400] *Jesuit Relations*, 2, pp. 93–95.

among the Iroquois should be assumed to imply its use as a substitute for human sacrifice. Furthermore, it was observed as early as sacrifice and may well have been older.

While the only cannibalism in the Southeast, that of the Southern Caddoans, gave evidence of having been acquired from the neighboring voracious man-eaters, that of the Iroquois had much resemblance to the eating of a sacrificial victim so prominent in Aztec human sacrifice ceremonials.[401] It has been suggested that the Aztec acquired a liking for human flesh through the religious compulsions to eat these victims,[402] and this might well have been true of the Iroquois. It must also be remembered that the Algonkians, such as the Miami and Shawnee, had Cannibalistic Societies to which captives were given, and the Sauk and Fox were said to have eaten captives at one time, all these cases presumably being without torturing.

Thus the Iroquois war trophy complex does not seem to have had any very close similarity with either the older Southeastern culture or with the intrusive Muskhogean culture. Caddoan-Iroquois relationships based on linguistic and presumed pottery resemblances are not confirmed by the war complex. On the contrary, it is very close to the typical Algonkian pattern. The exception to this would be torturing which, as has been suggested, was probably taken up by the Algonkians as a retaliatory measure against the Iroquois.

The Iroquois torture pattern had certain traits in common with human sacrifice in Mexico. These included cardiac emphasis, death by a knife, eating of the victims, and perhaps dancing and the use of a platform. None of these similarities, except possibly the dancing of the victim, are found associated with the frame torture of the lower Mississippi where Mexican resemblances were of an entirely different order. Furthermore, the evidence seems to point to a fairly recent accentuation of torturing by the Iroquois, as it apparently was not shared by the Cherokee until late wars with the Northern Iroquois, and had not diffused to the Algonkians much before the early white contacts.

[401] Sahagun, pp. 43, 52, 62, 75.
[402] Loeb, p. 11.

Southern Iroquois and Shawnee

Certain Southeastern tribes have not been classified under the three patterns as they seem to have occupied an intermediate position between the Northern Iroquois and the Muskhogean peoples to the south. Observations on these groups came relatively late and are very scanty.

The extremely warlike Shawnee obtained a reputation for cruelty but as has been indicated few descriptions of actual torturing are available.[403] Scalping was undoubtedly important although its significance is not known. Scalps were cleaned, dried, stretched on hoops and painted red.[404] A tradition obtained by Trowbridge from the Prophet mentions the scalping of a warrior by one of his own tribe. This scalp was later sent in a pot filled with blood to their enemies as a challenge for war.[404a] Cannibalism seems to have occurred only in connection with the Cannibalistic Society.

Many captives were adopted, perhaps the most famous being Daniel Boone who was their prisoner, and treated like a son, for several months in 1778.[405] Kenton was forced to run the gauntlet about that time. Six hundred Indians with sticks, tomahawks, and knives lined up for one-half a mile across a level plain and compelled Kenton to run between them to a council house.[406]

Torture among the Cherokee [407] was apparently influenced by the white pattern of burning at the stake and also by Iroquois methods. Here again the specific information is very scanty. It is also difficult to evaluate their treatment of captives. How extensive the holding of slaves was, before the development of the slave trade by the whites, is difficult to say. They kept many white prisoners as slaves after the war of 1760. These were said to have been the property of their individual captors.[408] Adoption was probably more customary than slavery on the aboriginal level, although there might always have remained the danger, to which Timberlake was exposed, of being killed to revenge depredations committed against the adoptors by rela-

---

403 See pp. 177 f.
404 Seaver, p. 48—Spencer, pp. 44 f.
404a Voegelin, p. 7.
405 Galloway, pp. 260–261.
406 Galloway, p. 256.
407 See pp. 176 f.
408 Timberlake, pp. 40, 90.

tives of a slain warrior.[409]   Captain Bonnefoy and four other Frenchmen, one a negro, were captured in 1741. They were well treated and adopted into families, except for the negro who was set free because he had been wounded. However, as he did not use his freedom, but continued to follow them, they gave him over to the young people who killed and scalped him. Before the adopted captives were permitted to enter the village they were compelled to sing for hours. Then they were tied together two by two and marched around a great tree in the village at the foot of which some of their hair was buried. They were then taken to the council house where each was made to sing four songs. After doing this they were washed and fed, and were then considered as brothers.[410]

Scalps were an important war trophy, so much so that they have been accused of killing one of their own tribe and pretending that the scalp was from a Shawnee.[411] A war party returned in 1761 with four painted Shawnee scalps on a pole which was carried three times around the Town House and then placed near the door.[412] Scalps were carried by women in the victory celebration held in the Town House.[413] Speck was told that the scalps had been carried by singing and dancing warriors in the Victory Dance, a part of the Eagle Dance, and afterwards collected by the leader and put carefully away.[414] Scalps were also said to have been carried on peace missions.[415]

There are no accounts of special purificatory rites upon the return from war. However, success in war, as in hunting, depended on the moral purity of the warrior.[416] Warriors underwent strenuous rites for strengthening their physical and spiritual powers under the guidance of the medicine men, and a certain class of consecrated warriors used no other weapon than the heavy oak or hickory war club.[417]

Practically nothing is known of the Tuscarora war trophy

[409] Timberlake, p. 84.
[410] Mereness, pp. 242–246.
[411] Mooney, *Myths,* pp. 375 f.
[412] Timberlake, p. 92.
[413] Mooney, *Myths,* p. 376.
[414] Speck, MS.
[415] Speck, MS.
[416] Logan, p. 26.
[417] Speck, MS.   The author is indebted to Dr. Frank G. Speck not only for full access to his valuable manuscript material but also for many suggestions and criticisms.

pattern except that they killed Lawson.[418] Captives were apparently given to the "priest" and the woman of highest rank, who compelled them to dance as a sign that they had become subjects. During the victory celebration each family occupied a separate scaffold which they had erected near the execution grounds. A fire was built near the scaffold and when a woman became tired of dancing she returned and sat on the scaffold to eat with her husband.[419]

V. Conclusions

1. *Frame Torture*

The Frame Torture of the lower Mississippi had many elements with sacrificial connotations. Such traits, however, were entirely distinct from those associated with the Iroquois torture pattern, and the resemblances with Mexico were consequently not parallel. Whether or not the use of a frame indicates relationship with Mexico is not obvious. Should this be so, the complex was probably acquired subsequently to 1506. Other indications of its relatively late appearance in this region are the absence of torture among the other peoples who were a part of the Older Southeastern Culture, the failure of Frame type torture to diffuse to contiguous tribes such as the Choctaw and Chickasaw, and the lack of reference to it in the chronicles of the De Soto expedition which do contain descriptions of human sacrifice of a different type. On the other hand, the emphasis upon war trophies, specifically scalps or "heads," as offerings to the supernatural and associated with the temples, and the importance of human sacrifice, not, however, connected with warfare, might well have evolved indigenously into the sacrifice of war captives. Whether the complex diffused essentially as such from Mexico or was of independent local growth from the same basic underlying concepts cannot be resolved until corroborative evidence is brought out by many detailed analyses of the cultures. The present evidence seems to favor the latter assumption. It may be fairly confidently asserted, nevertheless, that human sacrifice was the motivation for the Frame torturing of captives, and that there were no connections, except perhaps

[418] See p. 166.
[419] Graffenreid, Excerpts, Vol. I. Furnished through the kindness of Dr. John R. Swanton of the Bureau of American Ethnology who suggested many pertinent sources.

very remotely through a common Mexican origin, with the human sacrifice motive underlying Iroquois torture.

2. Pole and Stake Torture

Tortures in the Southeast which have been designated as Pole and Stake Torture strongly suggest a European origin. The absence of torturing among peoples of both the Old Southeastern Culture and the later Intrusive Culture until long after the first White contacts is indicated by the barrenness of the early sources, both in respect to positive descriptions and failure to suggest that the Indians had been feared because of the possibility of torture. When torture finally did get into the accounts almost 200 years after the arrival of the Europeans, it does not seem to have been integrated into the cultures or to have borne any religious or social connotations. Furthermore, the common European pattern of the stake heaped about with combustibles, unquestionably often inflicted upon recalcitrant Indians by the invaders, was used. Stake Torture was therefore based upon purely retaliatory motives and was a recently acquired reflection of the culture of Europe. It has been pointed out that the Pole Torture of the Chickasaw was probably of the same basic type as Stake Torture with possibly some Iroquoian influence.

3. Platform Torture

The Platform Torture of the Iroquois appears to have been based upon human sacrifice to the Sun or War God and to have had certain resemblances to Aztec sacrifice. The rest of the Iroquois war trophy pattern was very comparable to that of the surrounding Algonkians, who were apparently receiving the idea of torturing from the Iroquois and using it as a retaliatory measure. That the intensive practice of torture by the Northern Iroquois was of rather late growth is suggested by the probability that the Southern Iroquois did not use it until after comparatively late contact with the north and therefore it was not a part of the earlier combined culture. Furthermore, the penetration of torture into the Algonkian cultures was seemingly not deep and was recognized as being of Iroquois origin. Perhaps due to an upsurge of war interest the importance and numerical amount of human sacrifice, a very old complex, increased, thereby leading to a spread of terror of the Iroquois which was utilized and emphasized to obtain submission of their enemies with the consequent progressive brutalization of the human sacrifice motive.

It must be emphatically repeated that these conclusions can pretend to nothing more than a reasonable degree of probability based on the available material. Only through detailed studies of many other manifestations of Southeastern cultures will a clear understanding of the functional integrations emerge and the historical factors be properly evaluated. Such studies will obviously modify conclusions based on a limited segment of the cultures.

VI. Bibliography

ADAIR, JAMES. The History of the American Indians. London, 1775.

ALVORD, CLARENCE W., AND LEE BIDGOOD. First Explorations of the Trans-Allegheny Region by the Virginians, 1650–1674. Cleveland, 1912.

ARBER, EDWARD (Editor). Travels and Works of Captain John Smith, President of Virginia, and Admiral of New England. 1580–1631. Edinburgh, 1910.

BANDELIER, A. F. A. On the Art of War and Mode of Warfare of the Ancient Mexicans. Cambridge, 1877.

Final Report on the Investigations among the Indians of the Southwestern United States. Cambridge, 1890, 1892.

The Journey of Alvar Nunez Cabeza de Vaca. (Translated by F. Bandelier.) New York, 1905.

BARBEAU, C. M. Supernatural Beings of the Hurons and Wyandots. *American Anthropologist*, 16, 288–314, 1914.

Huron and Wyandot Mythology. (Canada Department of Mines—Geological Survey—Memoir 80, Anthropological Series 11, 1915.)

BARLOWE, CAPTAIN ARTHUR. The First Voyage made to the Coasts of America, 1584. (In ''Early English and French Voyages,'' Henry S. Burrage, Editor, New York, 1906.)

BARTRAM, WILLIAM. Observations on the Creek and Cherokee Indians, 1789. With Prefatory and Supplementary Notes by E. G. Squier. *Transactions of the American Ethnological Society*, 3, Pt. 1, New York, 1853.

Travels through North and South Carolina, Georgia, East and West Florida. . . . Philadelphia, 1791.

BEAUCHAMPS, WILLIAM A. A History of the New York Iroquois. New York State Museum, Bulletin 78, Archæology, 9, 1905.

Civil, Religious and Mourning Councils and Ceremonies of Adoption of the New York Indians. New York State Museum Bulletin 113, Archæology, 13, 1906.

BEVERLEY, ROBERT. The History of Virginia in Four Parts. Richmond, 1855. (Reprinted from the Author's Second Revised Edition, London, 1722.)

BIEDMA, LUIS HERNANDEZ DE. A Narrative of the Expedition of Hernando de Soto. (In French, 1850.)

BLAIR, EMMA HELEN. The Indian Tribes of the Upper Mississippi River Valley and the Region of the Great Lakes. 2 Vols. Cleveland, 1911.

BLAND, EDWARD AND OTHERS. The Discovery of New Brittaine, 1650. (In ''Narratives of Early Carolina,'' Alexander Salley, Editor, New York, 1911.)

BOSSU, M. Travels through that part of North America formerly called Louisiana. (Translated by J. R. Forster.) 2 Vols. London, 1771.

BUSHNELL, DAVID I., JR. Discoveries Beyond the Appalachian Mountains in September, 1671. *American Anthropologist*, 9, 45–63, 1907.

Virginia from Early Records. *American Anthropologist*, 9, 31–44, 1907.

Tribal Migrations east of the Mississippi. *Smithsonian Miscellaneous Collections*, 89, No. 12, 1934.

BRINTON, DANIEL G. Notes on the Floridian Peninsula, its Literary History, Indian Tribes and Antiquities. Philadelphia, 1859.

CARROLL, B. R. Historical Collections of South Carolina. Vols. I and II, New York, 1836.

CARTHIER, JACQUES. The First Relation of Jacques Carthier of S. Malo. (In ''Early English and French Voyages,'' Henry S. Burrage, Editor, New York, 1906.)

CHAMPLAIN, SAMUEL DE. The Works of Samuel de Champlain. Reprinted, Translated, and Annotated by Six Canadian Scholars under the General Editorship of H. P. Biggar. 6 Vols., Toronto, 1922–1936.

CHARLEVOIX, PIERRE FRANCOIS XAVIER DE. Historical Journal: in Letters Addressed to the Dutchess of Lesdiquieres. (In French, 1851.)

History and General Description of New France. (Edited by John Gilmary Shea.) 6 Vols., New York, 1900.

COLDEN, CADWALLADER. The History of the Five Indian Nations depending on the Province of New York. Reprinted exactly from Bradford's New York Edition (1727), New York, 1866.

CUSHMAN, HORATIO BARDWELL. History of the Choctaw, Chickasaw, and Natchez Indians. Greenville, Texas, 1899.

DORSEY, GEORGE A. The Mythology of the Wichita. Carnegie Institute of Washington, Publication No. 21, 1904.

DORSEY, J. OWEN. Omaha Sociology. 3rd. Annual Report, Bureau of American Ethnology, 1884.

DUMONT, M. History of Louisiana. Translated from the Historical Memoirs of M. Dumont. (In French, 1853.)

DUNBAR, JOHN B. The Pawnee Indians, their History and Ethnology. *Magazine of American History*, 4, No. 4; 5, No. 5, 1880.

DU PRATZ, LE PAGE. Historie de la Louisiane. Paris, 1758. 3 Vols.

EDGAR, MATILDA (Editor). Ten Years of Upper Canada. Toronto, 1890.

ELVAS, A Gentleman of. A Narrative of the Expedition of Hernando de Soto into Florida. Published at Eveva, 1557. Translated from the Portugese by Richard Hakluyt, London, 1609. (In French, 1850.)

FAIRBANKS, GEORGE R. The History and Antiquities of the City of St. Augustine, Florida. New York, 1858.

FENTON, WILLIAM N. An Outline of Seneca Ceremonies at Cold Spring Longhouse. Yale University Publications in Anthropology, No. 9, 1936.

FLANNERY, REGINA. An Analysis of Coastal Algonkian Culture. Catholic University of America, Anthropological Series No. 7, 1939.

FONTAINE, JAMES. Memoirs of a Huguenot Family. New York. Reprinted from the Original Edition of 1852.

FONTANEDA, HERNANDO DE ESCALANTE. Memoir of Hernando de Escalante Respecting Florida written in Spain about the Year 1575. (Translated from the Spanish by Buckingham Smith.) Washington, 1854.

FRENCH, B. F. Historical Collections of Louisiana. New York, 1846, 1850, 1851, 1853, 1869, 1875.

GALINEE, RENE DE BREHAUT DE. The Journey of Dollier and Galinee, 1669–1670. (In ''Early Narratives of the Northwest,'' Louise Phelps Kellogg, Editor, New York, 1917.)

GALLOWAY, WILLIAM ALBERT. Old Chillicothe-Shawnee and Pioneer History. Xenia, Ohio, 1934.

GAYARRE, CHARLES. History of Louisiana. 4 Vols., New York, 1854.

GRAFFENREID, DE. Ms. Excerpts copied for the Colonial Records of North Carolina from the Original MSS. in the Public Library at Yverdon, Switzerland.

HARIOT, THOMAS. A Brief and True Report of the New Found Land of Virginia. (A Facsimile Reproduction of the 1588 Quarto.) Ann Harbor, Michigan, 1931.

HARPE, BERNARD DE LA. Journal Historique de L'Establissements des Français a la Louisane. (In French, 1851.)

HATCHER, M. A. Description of the Tejas or Asinai Indians. *Southwestern Historical Quarterly*, **30, 31,** 1926–1928.

HAWKINS, BENJAMIN. A Sketch of the Creek Country in the Years 1798 and 1799. *Collections of the Georgia Historical Society*, **3,** Pt. 1, 1848.

Letters of Benjamin Hawkins, 1796–1806. *Collections of the Georgia Historical Society*, **9,** 1916.

HAY, HENRY. A Narrative of Life on the Old Frontier. *Proceedings of the Wisconsin State Historical Society*, 62nd. Annual Meeting, pp. 208–261, Madison, 1915.

HECKEWELDER, JOHN. History, Manners, and Customs of the Indian Nations who once Inhabited Pennsylvania and the Neighboring States. *Memoirs of the Historical Society of Pennsylvania*, **12,** 1876.

HENNEPIN, FATHER LOUIS. Account of the Discovery of the River Mississippi and the Adjacent Territory. (In French, 1846.)

HEWITT, J. N. B. The League of the Iroquois and its Constitution. Annual Report of the Smithsonian Institute, 1918.

White Dog Sacrifice. *Bulletin 30,* **2,** of the Bureau of American Ethnology.

HUNTER, JOHN D. Memoirs of a Captivity among the Indians of North America. London, 1824.

IBERVILLE, M. P. LeMOYNE D'. Narrative of the Voyage made by order of the King of France, in 1698, to take possession of Louisiana. (In French, 1869.)

Historical Journal, or Narrative of the Expeditions made to Colonize Louisiana under command of M. Pierre LeMoyne d'Iberville, Governor General. (In French, 1875.)

IMLAY, GILBERT. A Topographical Description of the Western Territory of North America. London, 1793.

JENNESS, DIAMOND. The Indians of Canada. Ottawa, 1932.

The Ojibwa Indians of Parry Sound, Their Social and Religious Life. Canada Department of Mines, Bull. 78, Anthropological Series, **17,** 1935.

Jesuit Relations and Allied Documents. Reuben Gold Thwaites, Editor, 73 Vols., Cleveland, 1897–1901.

JOUTEL, H. Historical Journal of Monsieur de la Salle's Last Voyage to discover the River Mississippi. (In French, 1846.)

Relation. (In Margry. Tome 3.)

KELLY, FANNY. Narrative of My Captivity among the Sioux Indians. Hartford, 1871.

LANE, RALPH. Account of the Particularities of the Employments of the Englishmen Left in Virginia, 1585–1586, by Master Ralph Lane. (In ''Early English and French Voyages,'' Henry S. Burrage, Editor, New York, 1906.)

LAUDONNIÈRE, RENE. A Notable Historie containing foure voyages made by certaine French Captains into Florida. (Translated out of French into English by M. Richard Hakluyt. In ''Voyages of the English Nation to America,'' **2,** Edinburgh, 1889.)

LAWSON, JOHN. History of Carolina, containing the exact description and natural history of that country. London, 1714.

LEDERER, JOHN. The Discoveries of John Lederer in three several marches. . . . Collected and translated by Sir William Talbot, Baronet. London, 1672. Reprinted, Rochester, N. Y. 1902.

LEETH, JOHN. A Short Biography of John Leeth with an account of his life among the Indians. Cleveland, 1904. (Reprinted from the Edition of 1831.)

LeMOYNE, JACQUES. Narrative of LeMoyne, an artist who accompanied the French Expedition to Florida under Laudonnière, 1564. Translated from the Latin of DeBry. Boston, 1875.

LINDESTROM, PETER. Geographia Americae with an Account of the Delaware Indians. Based on Surveys and Notes made in 1654–56. Philadelphia, 1925. (Translated by Amandas Johnson.)

LINTON, RALPH. The Origin of the Skidi Pawnee Sacrifice to the Morning Star. *American Anthropologist*, 28, No. 3, 1926.

LOEB, E. M. The Blood Sacrifice Complex. Memoir 30, American Anthropological Association, 1923.

LOGAN, JOHN H. A History of the Upper Country of South Carolina. Vol. I, Charleston and Columbia, 1859.

LOWERY, WOODBURY. The Spanish Settlements within the Present Limits of the United States, 1513–1561. New York, 1911.

The Spanish Settlements within the Present Limits of the United States: Florida, 1562–1574. New York, 1905.

MARGRY, PIERRE (Editor). Découvertes et Establissements des Français dans la Sud de l'Amerique Septentrionale (1614–1754). 6 Vols. Paris, 1877–1886.

MARQUETTE, PERE, AND SIEUR JOLIET. An Account of the Discovery of Some New Countries and Nations in North America in 1673. (In French, 1850.)

MARTYR, PETER (D'ANGHIERA). De Orbe Novo. English Translation by F. A. MacNutt. 2 Vols. New York, 1912.

MEGAPOLENSIS, REV. JOHANNES. A Short Account of the Mohawk Indians, 1644. (In ''Narratives of New Netherlands,'' J. Franklin Jameson, Editor, New York, 1909.)

MERENESS, NEWTON D. (Editor). Travels in the American Colonies. New York, 1916.

MILFORT, (LECLERC). Memoire ou coup-d'oeil rapide sur mes differens voyages et mon sejour dans la Nation Creek, Paris, 1802.

MOONEY, JAMES. Myths of the Cherokee. 19th. Annual Report, Pt. 1, Bureau of American Ethnology, 1900.

The Powhatan Confederacy, Past and Present. *American Anthropologist*, 9, 129–152, 1907.

MORFI, PADRE FRAY JUAN AGUSTIN DE. Excerpts from the Memorias for the History of the Province of Texas. Frederick C. Chabot, Editor, San Antonio, Texas, 1932.

MORGAN, LEWIS H. League of the Ho-De-No-Sau-Nee or Iroquois. 2 Vols. (in one). New York, 1904.

MURRAY, LOUISE WELLES (Editor). Selected Manuscripts of General John S. Clark Relating to the Aboriginal History of the Susquehanna. Athens, Pennsylvania, 1931.

PARKER, ARTHUR C. The Origin of the Iroquois as suggested by their Archæology. *American Anthropologist*, 18, No. 4, 1916.

PEARCE, JAMES E. Significance of the East Texas Archæological Field. (In ''Conference on Southern Pre-history,'' National Research Council, Washington, D. C., 1932, pp. 53–58.)

PENICAUT, M. Annals of Louisiana, 1698–1722. (In French, 1869.)

Relation. (In Margry, Tome 5.)

PERCY, GEORGE. Observations by Master George Percy, 1607. (In ''Early Narratives of Virginia,'' Lyon Gardiner Tyler, Editor, New York, 1907.)

POPE, JOHN. A Tour through the Northern and Western territories of the United States. Richmond, 1792.

RAMSEY, J. G. M. The Annals of Tennessee to the end of the Eighteenth Century, Philadelphia, 1853.

RANJEL, RODRIGO. A Narrative of de Soto's Expedition based on the Diary of Rodrigo Ranjel, his private Secretary, by Gonzalo Fernandez de Oviedo y Valdes. (In ''Narratives of the Career of Hernando de Soto,'' E. G. Bourne, 2, New York, 1904.)

RIBAULT, JOHN. The True and Last Discouerie of Florida made by Captain John Ribault in the Yeere 1562. (In Hakluyt Society Publications, 7, London, 1850.)

ROMANS, BERNARD. A Concise Natural History of East and West Florida, 1, New York, 1775.

Ru, Paul Du. Journal of a Voyage made with M. d'Iberville from Biloxi Bay up the Mississippi. (Translated from a Manuscript in The Newberry Library by Ruth Lapham Butler.) Chicago, 1934.

Sahagun, Fray Bernardino de. A History of Ancient Mexico. Translated by Fanny R. Bandelier, Nashville, Tennessee, 1932.

Schoolcraft, Henry R. Historical and Statistical Information respecting the History, Condition, and Prospects of the Indian Tribes of the United States. 6 Vols., Philadelphia, 1851–1857.

Seaver, James E. Life of Mary Jemison, Deh-he-wa-mis. New York, 1856.

Shetrone, Henry Clyde. The Mound Builders. New York, 1930.

Skinner, Alanson. War Customs of the Menomini Indians. American Anthropologist, 13, 299–312, 1911.

Observations on the Ethnology of the Sauk Indians. Bulletin of the Public Museum of Milwaukee, 5, 1–95, Pt. 2, 1925.

The Mascoutens or Prairie Potawatomi Indians. Bulletin of the Public Museum of Milwaukee, 6, Pt. 1, 1924.

Ethnology of the Ioway Indians. Bulletin of the Public Museum of Milwaukee, 5, Pt. 4, 1926.

Smith, Captain John. A True Relation—1608. (In "Narratives of Early Virginia," Lyon Gardiner Tyler, Editor, New York, 1907.)

A Map of Virginia, with a description of the Country. (In "Narratives of Early Virginia," Lyon Gardiner Tyler, Editor, New York, 1907.)

The Generall Historie of Virginia, New England and the Summer Isles—Book IV. (In "Narratives of Early Virginia," Lyon Gardiner Tyler, Editor, New York, 1907.)

Smith, Marian W. The War Complex of the Plains Indians. Proceedings of the American Philosophical Society, 78, No. 3, 1938.

Soto, Hernando de. Letter to the Municipal Authorities of St. Jago de Cuba, July, 1539. (In French, 1850.)

Speck, Frank G. Ethnology of the Yuchi Indians. Anthropological Publications of the University Museum, 1, Philadelphia, 1909.

Creek Indians of Taskigi Town. Memoir of the American Anthropological Association, 2, Pt. 2, 1907.

Spelman, Henry. Relation of Virginea. (In "Travels and Works of Captain John Smith." Edited by Edward Arber, Edinburgh, 1910.)

Spencer, O. M. Indian Captivity. New York, 1842.

Stirling, M. W. The Pre-historic Southern Indians. (In "Conference on Southern Pre-history," National Research Council, Washington, D. C., 1932, pp. 20–31.)

Strachey, William. The History of Travaile into Virginia Britania. Hakluyt Society Publications, 6, London, 1849.

Swan, Caleb. Position and State of Manners and Arts in the Creek, or Muskogee Nation in 1791. (In Schoolcraft, 5, 251–283.)

Swanton, John R. Indian Tribes of the Lower Mississippi Valley and Adjacent Coast of the Gulf of Mexico. Bulletin 43, Bureau of American Ethnology, 1911.

An Early Account of the Choctaw Indians. Memoir of the American Anthropological Association, 5, Pt. 2, 1918.

Early History of the Creek Indians. Bulletin 73, Bureau of American Ethnology, 1922.

Social Organization and Social Usages of the Indians of the Creek Confederacy. 42nd. Annual Report, Bureau of American Ethnology, 1928.

Religious Beliefs and Medical Practices of the Creek Indians. 42nd. Annual Report, Bureau of American Ethnolgoy, 1928.

Aboriginal Culture of the Southeast. 42nd. Annual Report, Bureau of American Ethnology, 1928.

Social and Religious Beliefs and Usages of the Chickasaw Indians. 44th. Annual Report, Bureau of American Ethnology, 1928.

Source Material for the Social and Ceremonial Life of the Choctaw Indians. Bulletin 103, Bureau of American Ethnology, 1931.

The Ethnological Value of the De Soto Narratives. *American Anthropologist,* **34,** 1932.

Southeastern Indians of History. (In ''Conference on Southern Pre-history,'' National Research Council, Washington, D. C., pp. 5–20, 1932.)

The Relation of the Southeast to General Culture Problems of American Pre-history. (In ''Conference on Southern Pre-history,'' National Research Council, Washington, D. C., pp. 60–74, 1932.)

THOMAS, CYRUS. Report on the Mound Explorations of the Bureau of Ethnology. 12th. Annual Report, Bureau of American Ethnology, 1894.

TIMBERLAKE, HENRY. The Memoirs of Lieut. Henry Timberlake, London, 1765.

TONTY, SIEUR DE LA. Memoir sent in 1693. (In French, 1846.)

Relation. (In Margry, Tome I, pp. 573–614.)

TROWBRIDGE, C. C. Meearmeear Traditions. Ann Arbor, Michigan, 1938.

UNKNOWN. Narrative of a Journey into the Mohawk and Oneida Country, 1634–35. (In ''Narratives of New Netherland,'' J. Franklin Jameson, Editor, New York, 1909.)

VEGA, GARCILASO DE LA. La Florida. (In ''The History of Hernando de Soto and Florida,'' Bernard Shipp, Philadelphia, 1881.)

VERARANUS, JOHN. Relation of John Veraranus. (In *Hakluyt Society Publications,* **7,** London, 1850.)

VOEGELIN, ERMINIE W., AND VERNON KINIETZ. Shawnese Traditions, C. C. Trowbridge's Account. Ann Arbor, 1939.

WASSENAER, NICHOHAES VAN. Historisch Verhael. (In ''Narratives of New Netherland,'' J. Franklin Jameson, Editor, New York, 1909.)

WENHOLD, LUCY L. A 17th. Century Letter of Gabriel Diaz Vara Calderon, Bishop of Cuba, Describing the Indians and Indian Missions of Florida. *Smithsonian Miscellaneous Collections,* **95,** No. 16, 1936.

WHITE, JOHN. The Fourth Voyage made to Virginia with three ships, in yere 1587. Wherein was transported the second Colonie. (In ''Voyages of the English Nation to America,'' Hakluyt, **2,** 1889.)

The fift voyage of M. John White into the West Indies and parts of America called Virginia, in the yere 1590. (In ''Voyages of the English Nation to America,'' Hakluyt, **2,** 1889.)

WILLIAMSON, HUGH. History of North Carolina. 2 Vols., Philadelphia, 1812.

WINSOR, JUSTIN. Narrative and Critical History of America. Vols. I–VIII. Boston and New York, 1884–1889.

WISSLER, CLARK, AND H. J. SPINDEN. The Pawnee Human Sacrifice to the Morning Star. *American Museum Journal,* **16,** 1916.

ZEISBERGER, DAVID. History of the Northern American Indians. *Ohio State Archæological and Historical Society,* 1910.